SAMSUNG G

A15 5G USER GUIDE

THE COMPLETE, STEP-BY-STEP, AND ILLUSTRATIVE MANUAL WITH TIPS AND TRICKS FOR BEGINNERS AND SENIORS TO QUICKLY MASTER THEIR NEW DEVICE LIKE A PRO

Benjamin Israel

Copyright © 2024 **Benjamin Israel**

Disclaimer: This book is not the official Samsung Galaxy manual. The images used in this manual are only for illustrative purposes; all information is deemed accurate and meant to assist the reader/user. The author/publisher shall not be liable for any misuse, abuse, damage, or loss arising from applying any of the contents in this manual. Please contact the carrier or manufacturer of your device if you have any queries or concerns.

All rights reserved. This book is copyright and no part of it may be reproduced, distributed, or transmitted in any form or by any means, including photocopying, recording, or other electronic or mechanical methods, without the prior written permission of the publisher, except in the case of brief quotations embodied in critical reviews and certain other noncommercial uses permitted by copyright law.

Printed in the United States of America

Copyright © 2024 **Benjamin Israel**

Contents

- INTRODUCTION 1
- Chapter One 2
- GETTING STARTED 2
  - Features and their functions 2
  - Physical (Hard) buttons and their functions 5
    - How to set the Side button 5
  - Soft buttons and their functions 6
  - How to charge the battery 7
    - Wired charging 7
    - Quick charging 7
    - How to charge other devices 8
    - How to reduce the battery consumption 8
    - Battery charging tips and precautions 9
  - How to install a nano-SIM card 10
    - Steps for installing the SIM or USIM card 11
    - SIM card manager (dual SIM models) 13
  - How to insert an SD card 14

How to safely remove an SD card from your Galaxy A15 5G 16

Formatting the microSD card 17

How to turn on/off the Galaxy A15 5G 18

Forcing restart 19

Emergency mode 19

Chapter Two 21

HOW TO SET UP YOUR PHONE 21

Initial setup 21

How to set up Samsung account on your Galaxy A15 5G 21

How to Find your ID and reset your password 22

Signing out of your Samsung account 22

How to transfer data from your previous device to your new Galaxy A15 5G (using Smart Switch) 23

Transferring data using a USB cable 23

How to Transfer your data wirelessly 24

How to use external storage to backup and restore data 26

How to transfer backup data from a computer to your new Galaxy A15 5G 26

How to install or uninstall apps on your new Galaxy A15 5G 27

    Galaxy Store 27

    Play Store 28

    Managing apps 28

Chapter Three 30

HOW TO SETUP AND MANAGE YOUR SECURITY AND PRIVACY FEATURES ON YOUR NEW PHONE 30

Face recognition 30

Fingerprint recognition 33

Extend Unlock 38

Secure Folder 39

    Secure Wi-Fi 44

Samsung Pass 46

Chapter Four 51

GETTING USED TO YOUR PHONE'S FEATURES AND FUNCTIONS 51

   Understanding the screen 51

      Navigation bar (soft buttons) 52

      Home screen and Apps screen 53

      Edge panel 59

      Lock screen 59

      Indicator icons 60

   Notification panel 62

      Using quick setting buttons 63

      Controlling media playback 64

Chapter Five 65

COMMUNICATIONS 65

   The Phone app 65

      Making calls 65

      Receiving calls 67

      Blocking phone numbers 67

      Things you can do during a call. 68

   The Contacts app 70

How to save contacts to your Galaxy A15 5G 70

How to find contacts on your phone 71

Sharing contacts 72

Creating groups 72

How to merge duplicate contacts 72

The Messages app 72

How to enter text... 73

Copying and pasting 74

Sending messages 76

Viewing messages 76

Changing message settings 77

Internet 77

Using secret mode 79

Chapter Six 80

THE CAMERA AND GALLERY APPS 80

Camera 80

How to take pictures with your phone 80

How to use the Photo mode on Galaxy A15 5G 87

- Video mode 88
- Portrait mode 89
- Fun mode 90
- Pro mode 91
- Night mode 93
- Food mode 93
- Panorama mode 93
- Macro mode 94
- Slow motion mode 94
- Hyperlapse mode 95
- Customizing camera settings 96

Screenshotting and screen recording 99
- How to capture a screenshot 99
- Screen record 101

Gallery 101
- Using Gallery 102
- Viewing images 102
- How to crop enlarged images in Gallery 103
- Viewing videos 103

Albums 104

Stories 105

How to Sync images and videos on your device with your cloud account 105

Deleting images or videos 106

AR Zone 106

Learn how to launch and use the AR Zone 106

Learn about AR Emoji Studio 107

Making an AR emoji short video and using it to decorate your device. 108

Using an AR emoji to create your contact profile. 109

Working with AR Emoji Stickers 110

Chapter Seven 112

GALAXY APPS AND FEATURES 112

Samsung Health 112

Using Samsung Health 112

Samsung Notes 114

Creating notes 114

Samsung Kids 115

How to use the parental control features .. 115
Closing Samsung Kids 116
Galaxy Wearable 116
Calendar 116
Creating events 116
Syncing events with your accounts 117
Reminder 117
Starting Reminder 118
Creating reminders 118
Completing reminders 118
Deleting reminders 119
Voice Recorder 119
Changing the recording mode on the Galaxy A15 5G 119
How to listen to radio on your phone 120
How to use the My Files app 121
Gaming Hub 121
Removing a game from Gaming Hub 122
Changing the performance mode 122
Game Booster 122

Launching apps in pop-up windows while playing games 124

Google apps 125

Chapter Eight 127
CONNECTIONS AND SHARING 127

Wi-Fi 127

Bluetooth 129

NFC and contactless payments 131

Data saver 134

Allowed network for apps 134

Mobile Hotspot 135

More connection settings 136

Printing 137

Different ways to share content on your Galaxy A15 smartphone. 138

How to use the Quick Share 138

Music Share 141

How to share your Bluetooth speaker with another device 141

Listening to music together with Galaxy Buds 142

SmartThings 143

Smart View 144

Chapter Nine 146

CUSTOMIZATION SETTINGS 146

Samsung account 146

Notifications 146

Display settings 147

Home screen 149

    Motion smoothness 149

    How to change the screen mode or adjust the display color: 150

Wallpaper 152

Themes 152

Sounds and vibration 152

    Options 152

    Sound quality and effects. 154

    Separate app sound 154

Chapter Ten 156

ACCOUNTS AND BACKUP 156

Samsung Cloud 157

Chapter Eleven 159

ADVANCED SETTINGS 159

Advanced features 159

Motions and gestures 160

Video call effects 161

Dual Messenger 162

Digital Wellbeing and parental controls 163

Battery and device care 164

Optimizing your device 164

Battery 165

Storage 166

Memory 166

App protection 167

Maintenance mode 167

How to use the Ultra data saving mode 167

Apps 168

General management 168

Adding device languages 169
Accessibility 170
Software update 171
Security updates information 171
About phone 171
Chapter Twelve 173
TROUBLESHOOTING TIPS 173
Restarting the device 175
Forcing restart 175
Resetting the device 175
Removing the battery 181
INDEX 182

INTRODUCTION

*C*ongratulations on your purchase of the new Samsung Galaxy A15 5G smartphone! And welcome to the Galaxy Family", if this is your first Galaxy phone!!

The Samsung Galaxy A15 5G smartphone is a budget smartphone that ensures no one is left behind the trail of technological innovations and advancement in nowadays smartphones.

So, whether you use your smartphone for business, communication, browsing the internet, or simply to stay in touch with friends and family, the Galaxy A15 5G is adequately equipped to handle your needs.

With an impressive 6.5" and a Super AMOLED display, a massive 5,000mAh battery that supports Supper Fast Charging, a powerful processing power, ample memory and storage options, and 5G speed, the Galaxy A15 is a smartphone to reckon with.

This complete step-by-step guide will help you get started and master all the features, settings, and functions of your Galaxy A15 5G smartphone like a pro in the easiest way possible.

So, relax and let's get started.

Chapter One
GETTING STARTED

Features and their functions

- Microphone
- SIM card / microSD card tray
- Light sensor
- Volume button
- Front camera
- Side button (Fingerprint recognition sensor)
- Touch screen
- Headphone jack
- Multipurpose jack (USB Type-C)
- Flash
- GPS antenna
- Rear camera
- NFC antenna (NFC-enabled models)
- Main antenna
- Speaker
- Microphone

Be cautious of the following:

- When using the speakers, such as when playing media files or using speakerphone, do not put the device near your ears.
- Take care not to expose the camera lens to a strong light source, such as direct sunlight as this may damage the camera image sensor. A damaged image sensor cannot be repaired and will produce dots or spots in pictures.
- If the device's glass or acrylic body is broken, take the device to a Samsung Service Centre for repairs before using it to avoid the risk of injury.
- If dust or foreign materials enter the microphone, speaker, or receiver, the device's sound may be impaired or certain features may not work. Attempting to remove the dust or foreign materials with a sharp object may cause damage to the device and affect its appearance.

Take note of the following:

- Connectivity problems and battery drain may ensue in the following circumstances:

- Attaching metallic stickers on the antenna area of the device.
- Attaching a device cover made with metallic material to the device.
- Shielding the device's antenna area with your hands or other objects as you're using certain features, such as calls or the mobile data connection.

• It is advisable to use a Samsung-endorsed screen protector. The use of unapproved screen protectors may cause malfunctioning of the sensors.

• Never cover the light sensor area with screen accessories, such as a screen protector, stickers, or a cover as doing so may cause the sensor to malfunction.

Physical (Hard) buttons and their functions

Side button
- Turn the phone on or off by pressing and holding this button for a few seconds.
- Press the button to turn on or lock the screen.
- Double press the button to open any app or feature you have set to work that way.

Side button + Volume Down button
- Press both buttons simultaneously to take a screenshot.
- Press and hold both buttons simultaneously for a few seconds to power off the device.

How to set the Side button

Choose the action to perform (e.g. an app or feature you want to open) anytime you double press the Side button or whenever you press down (i.e. press and hold) the Side button.

To do this, go to **Settings**, select **Advanced features**, select **Side button**, and then choose an option you want.

Soft buttons and their functions

The soft buttons are the navigation buttons that appear at the bottom of your device's screen whenever you turn it on.

Recents button ——— Back button

Home button

They give the user direction while operating the device, hence also called navigation buttons. As can be seen from the screenshot above, they are set to display the **Recents** button (left), **Home** button (center), and the **Back** button (right) on the navigation bar by default. However, you can also rearrange how they appear on the screen if you wish.

Their functions vary from one app to another and as well as the usage environment. Below is an illustration of their general functions.

| Recents button ||| | • Tap it to open the list of recent apps. |

| Home button ⬜ | • Tap to return to the Home screen.
• Touch and hold to launch the Google Assistant app. |

| Back button ‹ | • Tap to return to the previous screen |

6

How to charge the battery

Charge the battery before using it for the first time or when it has been unused for prolonged periods.

Wired charging

Connect the device's USB cable to the USB power adaptor and plug the cable into the device's multipurpose jack to charge the battery. After the device is fully charged, disconnect the charger from the device.

USB power adapter
USB cable

Quick charging

For quick charging, use a fast or super-fast charger.

To see if the charger is properly connected, go to **Settings** and tap **Battery**.

• If fast charging is not working, go to **Settings** > **Battery** > **Charging settings**. Confirm that the USB cord and the USB power adapter are securely connected as well.

- You can make the battery charge faster if you switch off the phone or its screen.

How to charge other devices

You can charge another mobile device with your phone's battery using the USB cable.

Simply connect your phone and the other device using the USB cable that came with your phone.

When charging begins, the battery charging icon appears on the screen of the other device.

The app selection pop-up window that displays on your smartphone is meant for data transfer. Selecting an app from the pop-up window is not advised.

How to reduce the battery consumption

Your smartphone offers various options that can help you save battery power. These include:

- Activating the power saving mode.
- Enhancing the device using the device care feature.
- Turning off the screen by pressing the Side button when the device is not being used.
- Closing any unnecessary apps.
- Deactivating the Bluetooth feature when you're not using it.

- Reducing the backlight time.
- Reducing the screen brightness.
- Deactivating auto-syncing of apps which require syncing.

Battery charging tips and precautions

- If the battery is totally discharged, the device cannot be turned on instantly when the charger is connected. Allow an empty battery to charge for a few minutes before you turn on the device.
- If you use multiple apps at once, network apps, or apps that need a connection to another device, the battery will empty quickly. To avoid losing power during a data transfer, always use these apps after you've fully charged the battery.
- The charging speed of your device may reduce when you're charging it with other sources of power, e.g. a computer due to a lower electric current.
- The device can be used while charging, but it the battery may take longer time to get fully charged.

- If the device receives an unsteady power supply while charging, the touch screen may not work. In that case, disconnect the charger from the device.
- While charging, the device and the charger may become hot. This is normal and does not affect the device's lifespan or performance. However, if the battery gets hotter than normal, the charger may stop charging.
- If the multipurpose jack is wet and you use it to charge, it may cause damage to the device.
  Always ensure the multipurpose jack is dry before charging the device.
- If the device is not charging appropriately, take the device and its charger to a Samsung Service Centre.

How to install a nano-SIM card

Insert the SIM or USIM card supplied by your service provider.

In some locations, using dual SIM card may result in reduced speeds when transferring data.

NOTE: Some services requiring a network connection may be unavailable depending on the service provider.

Steps for installing the SIM or USIM card

Ejection pin

Single SIM card tray

Dual SIM card tray

<Underside>

1. Push the ejection pin into the hole on the tray to bring out the tray.
2. Gently pull out the tray from the tray slot.
3. Put the SIM or USIM card on the tray with the gold-colored contacts facing upwards and gently press the SIM or USIM card into the tray to make it is firm.
4. Carefully insert the tray back into the tray slot.

CAUTION:

- Press the ejection pin into the **tray's hole** to expose the tray.
- Use only a nano-SIM card.
- Be cautious not to lose your SIM or USIM card, or allow others have unauthorized access to it. Samsung does not accept any legal responsibility for any damages or inconveniences experience because of lost or stolen cards.
- Check to ascertain hat the ejection pin is perpendicular to the hole. Or else, the device may be damaged.
- If you do not fix the SIM card firmly into the tray, it may fall out of the tray unawares.
- If you insert a wet tray into your device, your device may get damaged. Always make sure the tray is dry before inserting it into your device.
- Ensure the tray is completely inserted into the tray slot to prevent liquid from entering your device.

How to correctly install SIM card (dual SIM card tray)

SIM1 — SIM
SIM2 — microSD card
<Underside> <Underside>

SIM card manager (dual SIM models)

Open the **Settings** app, then tap **Connections**, and tap **SIM manager**.

- **SIM cards**: Activate the SIM card to start using it and customize the SIM card settings.

- **Preferred SIM card**: Choose which specific SIM cards you would want to use for some features, such as voice calls, when two cards are activated.

- **Data switching:** Set the phone to automatically switch to using the second SIM card for data services when the preferred SIM card is unable to connect to the network.

- **More SIM settings**: Customize the call settings.

How to insert an SD card

The maximum capacity of the SD card your device can hold may differ from other models'. Some SD cards may have incompatibility issues with your smartphone, depending on the manufacturer and type of the SD card. To know your device's SD memory card capacity, please visit the Samsung website.

1. Safely insert the ejection pin into the hole on the tray to release the tray.
2. Pull out the tray from the tray slot with caution.

<Underside>

3 Put a memory card on the tray with the gold-colored contacts facing upwards and gently press the memory card into the tray to make it firm.

4 Insert the tray back into the tray slot carefully.

CAUTION:

- Press the ejection pin into the **tray's hole** to expose the tray.
- Some memory cards may not be wholly compatible with the device. Using a memory card that is not compatible with your device result in damage to the device or the memory card or corrupt the data you have stored in them.
- Carefully insert the memory card right-side up.
- Confirm that the ejection pin is perpendicular to the hole. Or else, the device may get damaged.
- Removing the tray from the device disables the mobile data connection.
- If you don't fix the card firmly into the tray, the memory card may leave or fall out of the tray.
- If you insert a wet tray into your device, the device may be damaged. Always make sure the tray is dry before inserting it into your device.

- Be cautious to insert the tray completely into the tray slot to avoid liquid from entering your device.

NOTE:
- The device complies with the FAT and the exFAT file systems for SD cards. When you insert an SD card that has been formatted in a different file system into your device, it will request you to format the card again in your device or else, it will not identify the card. To use the SD card, you must first of all format it. If your device cannot format or identify the memory card, contact the SD card manufacturer or a Samsung Service Centre.
- Frequent writing and erasing of data reduce the lifespan of memory cards.
- When inserting an SD card into your smartphone, you'll see the SD card's file directory in the **My Files** > **SD card** folder.

How to safely remove an SD card from your Galaxy A15 5G

Before you take out the SD card, you must first unmount it.

Open the **Settings** app and tap **Device care,** then select **Storage.** Swipe to the left to display the **SD card** page. Then tap **More options** ⋮ and tap **Unmount.**

CAUTION: Never remove external storage, such as a memory card or USB storage, while the device is transferring or accessing information, or right after transferring data. Doing so may lead to data corruption or loss or cause damage to the external storage or device. Samsung is not responsible for losses, including data loss, that happen when external storage devices are used in the wrong way.

Formatting the microSD card

A microSD card that has been formatted on a computer may not be compatible with the device. It is recommended that you format the SD card on the device.

Open the **Settings** app and tap **Device care** > **Storage.** Swipe to the left to display the **SD card** page, tap **More options** ⋮ and then tap **Format.**

CAUTION: Before you format the memory card, remember to make backup copies of all important data stored in the memory card. Loss of data resulting from user actions is not covered in the manufacturer's warranty.

How to turn on/off the Galaxy A15 5G

To turn on your device, simply **press and hold the Side button for a few seconds**.

When it comes to turning off your phone, there are several ways to do that. Below are three methods you can use to power off your Galaxy A15 5G phone.

1. Press and hold the **Side button** for a few seconds. The Power menu will appear on the screen. Tap the **Power off** option.

2. The second method is to swipe down twice from the top of the screen, or swipe downwards with your two fingers from the top of the screen, tap the Power off icon ⏻ at the top right

corner of the screen to bring up the Power menu, and then tap the **Power off** option.

3. The last option is to ask **Bixby** to turn off the phone for you.

NOTE: If you want to restart the device, tap **Restart** when the power menu appears on the screen.

Forcing restart

If your device becomes frozen and unresponsive, press and hold the Side key and the Volume Down key simultaneously for a period longer than 7 seconds to restart it.

Emergency mode

You may switch the device to emergency mode to reduce battery consumption. Some apps and functions will be limited. In emergency mode, you can make an emergency call, send your current location information to others, sound an emergency alarm, etc. with your device.

To activate the Emergency mode in your device, press and hold the **Side button**, then tap **Emergency call**. In the alternative, you can also open the notification panel, swipe downwards, tap ⏻, and then tap **Emergency call**.

NOTE: You can edit your medical information and emergency contacts by navigating to **Settings > Safety and emergency.**

Chapter Two
HOW TO SET UP YOUR PHONE

Initial setup

When you turn on your Galaxy phone for the first time or after performing a data reset, make sure to follow the on-screen instructions to set up your device.

NOTE: Unless you connect to a Wi-Fi network, you may not be able to set up some device features during the initial setup.

How to set up Samsung account on your Galaxy A15 5G

Your Samsung account is an integrated account service that lets you use several of Samsung services offered on mobile devices, TVs, and the Samsung website.

To see the list of services that can be used with your Samsung account, please visit account.samsung.com.

1. Go to the **Settings** app, tap **Accounts and backup > Manage accounts > Add account > Samsung account**.

    Alternatively, open the **Settings** menu and tap **Samsung account**.

2. If you already have an existing Samsung account, sign in to your account. If not, tap "**Forgot password or don't have an account?**", and then tap **Create account** to sign up for a Samsung account,

How to Find your ID and reset your password

If you ever forget your Samsung account ID or password, tap "**Forgot password or don't have an account?**", select either **Forgot ID** (to find your ID) or **Forgot password** (to reset your password) on the Samsung account sign-in screen. However, you'll need to provide some important information before you can successfully recover your ID or reset your password.

Signing out of your Samsung account

Any time you sign out of your Samsung account, your data, such as contacts or events, will also be removed from your device.

1. From your **Settings** menu, tap **Accounts and back-up**, then **Manage accounts**.
2. Tap **Samsung** account, then go to **My profile** and tap **Sign out** which can be found at the bottom of the screen.
3. Tap **Sign out**, then input your Samsung account password, and tap **OK**.

How to transfer data from your previous device to your new Galaxy A15 5G (using Smart Switch)

You can use Smart Switch to transfer data from your old device to your new phone. Go to the **Settings** menu and tap **Accounts and backup > Bring data from old device**.
NOTE:
- This feature may not be available on some devices or computers.
- Restrictions apply. Please visit www.samsung.com/smartswitch for details. Samsung takes copyright as sacrosanct. You should only transfer content that you own or have the right to transfer.

Transferring data using a USB cable

You can connect your old device to your device with the USB cable to transfer your data seamlessly and quickly.

1 Connect your new Galaxy A15 5G phone and the previous device using your phone's USB cable. You may need a USB connector depending on your old device.
2 When the app selection pop-up window displays, tap **Smart Switch > Receive data**.

3   On your old device, tap **Allow**.

   If you do not have the app, download it from **Galaxy Store** or **Play Store**.

   Your device will automatically recognize the previous device and display a list of data you can transfer.

4   On your Galaxy A15 5G phone, choose an option and tap **Next**, and then follow the onscreen instructions to complete transferring the data.

CAUTION: Never disconnect the USB cable from the device when you are transferring files. Doing so may cause data loss or damage your device.

NOTE: Transferring data increases the rate of battery power consumption by your device. Make sure your device is well charged before transferring data. Low battery power may cause interruption of data transfer.

How to Transfer your data wirelessly

Transfer data from your previous device to your new Galaxy A15 5G wirelessly via Wi-Fi Direct by following the simple steps:

1   Launch the **Smart Switch** app on your old phone.

   If you do not have the app in the phone, download it from **Galaxy Store** or **Play Store**.

2   On your new phone, go to the **Settings** and tap **Accounts and backup** > **Bring data from old device**.

3   Place the two phones close to each other.

4   On your old phone, tap **Send data,** then select **Wireless**.

5   On your new phone, tap **Receive data**. Select the operating system (e.g. Android or iOS) of your old device and tap **Wireless.**

6   On your old phone, tap **Allow.**

7   On your new Galaxy A15 phone, select an option and tap **Next**. Follow the onscreen steps to complete transferring data.

How to use external storage to backup and restore data.

Transfer data using external storage, such as a microSD (memory) card.

1. Back up data from your old device to external storage.
2. Insert or make a connection between the external storage device and your smartphone.
3. On your smartphone, go to **Settings** and tap **Accounts and backup,** and select **External storage transfer**.
4. Select the backup data under **Restore from,** select the option you want to use and tap **Next**.
5. Follow the on-screen instructions to transfer your data.

How to transfer backup data from a computer to your new Galaxy A15 5G

You can transfer the data you've backed up on a computer from your old device to your new smartphone. However, you must first download the Smart Switch computer version app from www.samsung.com/smartswitch. To do this, follow the steps below:

1. Go to www.samsung.com/smartswitch on your computer to download **Smart Switch**.
2. Launch the **Smart Switch** app on your computer.

> **NOTE:** If your previous device is not a Samsung device, then you've got to back up your data to a computer using a program provided by the device's manufacturer. Then, skip to the fifth step.

3. Now, connect your previous device to the computer with its USB cable.
4. Follow the on-screen instructions on the computer to back up your data from the device.
5. After backing up your data, disconnect your old device from the computer.
6. Now, connect your new Galaxy phone to the computer using the USB cable.
7. On the computer, follow the on-screen instructions to transfer data to your new phone.

How to install or uninstall apps on your new Galaxy A15 5G

Galaxy Store

Buy and download apps. You can download apps that are tailored to Samsung Galaxy devices.

Launch the **Galaxy Store** app. Surf apps by category or tap the **Search** icon Q to search for keywords.

NOTE:

- This app may not be present depending on the service provider or model.
- To modify the auto update settings, tap **Menu,** tap the **Settings cog** ⚙ and then tap **Auto update apps**, and then select an option.

Play Store

Buy and download apps.

Launch the **Play Store** app. Surf apps by category or search for apps by keyword.

NOTE: To modify the auto update settings, tap the icon for your account, the go to **Settings** > **Network Preferences** > **Auto-update apps**, and then pick from the available options.

Managing apps

Uninstalling or disabling apps

Tap and hold an app and select from the options:

- **Uninstall**: Uninstall downloaded apps.
- **Disable**: Disable marked default apps that cannot be uninstalled from the device.

NOTE: Some apps may not function with this feature.

Enabling apps

Launch the **Settings** app, tap **Apps** > ⋮≡ > **Disabled** > **OK**, choose the app you want, and then tap **Enable**.

How to set app permissions

For some apps to function well, they may request permission to access or use information on your device.

To see your app permission settings, launch the **Settings** app and tap **Apps**. Pick an app and tap **Permissions**. You can peruse the app's permissions list and change its permissions.

To display or modify app permission settings by permission category, launch the **Settings** app and tap **Apps** > ⋮ > **Permission manager**. Select what you want and choose an app.

NOTE: Unless you grant permissions to apps, the basic features of the apps may not work optimally.

Chapter Three

HOW TO SETUP AND MANAGE YOUR SECURITY AND PRIVACY FEATURES ON YOUR NEW PHONE

Face recognition

You can configure your phone to unlock the screen by simply recognizing your face.

NOTE:

- If you use your face as a screen lock method, your face cannot be used to unlock the screen for the first time you turn on your phone. To use the phone, you must first unlock the screen using the pattern, PIN, or password that you set when registering the face. Be mindful never to forget your pattern, PIN, or password.
- If you change the screen lock method to **Swipe** or **None**, which are not recommended, all your biometric data will be removed. If you choose to use your biometric data in apps or features, you must re-register your biometric data.

Precautions for using face recognition.

Before using the face recognition to unlock your device, remember the following precautions:

- Someone or something else that looks like your image could be able to unlock your device.
- Face recognition is not as secure as Pattern, PIN, or Password.

Tips for better face recognition

Bear in mind the foollowing when using face recognition:

- Consider the circumstances under which you're registering, such as wearing glasses, hats, masks, beards, or heavy makeup.
- Make sure you're in a well-lit area and that the camera lens is clean when registering.
- Be sure your image is not blurry for better match results.

How to register your face

For a more accurate face registration, register your face indoors and avoid direct sunlight.

1. From the Settings screen, click **Security and privacy,** select **Biometrics,** and then select **Face recognition**.
2. Read the on-screen instructions and click **Continue**.

3   Set your preferred screen lock method.
4   Position your face inside the frame on the screen to enable the camera to scan your face.

NOTE:
- If unlocking the screen with your face is not working appropriately, click **Remove face data** to remove your registered face and register your face again.
- To improve the face recognition, click the option that says, "**Add alternative appearance to enhance recognition**" and add an alternate appearance.

How to unlock the screen with your face

You can use your face to unlock your phone's screen instead of using a pattern, PIN, or password.

1. Go to the Settings screen, click **Security and Privacy,** select **Biometrics,** and the select **Face recognition.**
2. Unlock the screen by simply using the preset screen lock method.
3. Click the **Face unlock** switch to activate the feature.
4. On the locked screen, look directly at the screen.

If it recognizes your face, you can unlock the screen without using any extra screen lock method. If your face is not recognized, then you must use the preset screen lock method.

How to delete the registered face data

You can remove face data that you have registered.
1. From the Settings screen, tap **Security and Privacy,** select **Biometrics,** and the select **Face recognition.**
2. Unlock the screen by simply using the current screen lock method.
3. Click **Remove face data,** and then click **Remove.**
As soon as the registered face is deleted, all other related features will also be deactivated.

Fingerprint recognition

Before you can use fingerprint recognition, you must first register and save your fingerprint information in your device.

NOTE:
- Availability of this feature depends on the service provider or model.
- Fingerprint recognition uses the unique characteristics of each fingerprint to increase the security of your

device. The likelihood of the fingerprint sensor confusing two different fingerprints is very minimal. Nevertheless, in rare occasions where separate fingerprints are very similar, the sensor may recognize them as alike.

- If you use a screen protector, ensure it permits for use of the On-screen fingerprint sensor.
- If you use your fingerprint as a screen lock method, you will not be able to use it to unlock the screen for the first time after turning on the device. To use the device, you must first unlock the screen using the pattern, PIN, or password you set during the registration of the fingerprint. Be cautious not to forget your pattern, PIN, or password.
- If the device does not recognize your fingerprint, unlock the device using the pattern, PIN, or password you set during the registration of the fingerprint, and then register your fingerprints again. If you forget your pattern, PIN, or password, you will not be able to use the device unless you reset it. Samsung is not accountable for any loss of data or inconvenience that may be caused by forgotten unlock codes.

- If you change the screen lock method to **Swipe** or **None**, which are less secure, all your biometric data will be deleted from the device. If you want to use your biometric data in apps or features, you must first re-register your biometric data.

Tips for better fingerprint recognition

When you scan your fingerprints on your Galaxy A15 5G phone, be conscious of the following conditions that may affect the feature's performance:

- The device may not be able to recognize fingerprints if they are affected by wrinkles or scars.
- The device may not recognize fingerprints from fingers that are too small or thin.
- To improve recognition performance, register fingerprints of the hand that is most often used to operate the device.
- There is a built-in fingerprint recognition sensor at the bottom center of your device's screen. Make sure that you secure the screen protector or the touch screen on the fingerprint recognition sensor area from scratches or damages by objects, such as coins, keys, pens, and necklaces.

- Make sure that the fingerprint recognition sensor area right at the bottom center of the screen and your fingers are clean and dry when fingerprinting.
- If your finger is not placed properly on the surface of the fingerprint recognition area, the device may not recognize your fingerprints. Avoid bending your finger or using a fingertip. Press the screen tightly with your finger in a way that your fingertip spreads over the wide surface of the fingerprint recognition area.

How to register your fingerprints

1 Open **Settings**, go to **Security and Privacy**, select **Biometrics**, and then select **Fingerprints**.

2 Read the on-screen instructions and click **Continue**.

3 Set a preferred screen lock method.

4 Click **Register** and Position your finger on the fingerprint recognition sensor. When the device detects

36

your finger, pull it up and place it on the fingerprint recognition sensor again.

Repeat the process until the fingerprint is completely registered.

5   When you are done registering your fingerprints, click the **Done** button.

You can check whether your fingerprint is registered by clicking **Check added fingerprints**.

How to unlock the screen with your fingerprints

You can unlock your phone's screen with your fingerprint if you do not want to use a pattern, PIN, or password.

1   Open to the Settings screen, click **Security and Privacy,** select **Biometrics,** and the select **Fingerprints**.

2   Unlock the screen by using the current screen lock method.

3   Press the **Fingerprint unlock** switch to turn it on.

4   On the locked screen, put your finger on the fingerprint recognition sensor and scan your fingerprint.

How to delete registered fingerprints

Follow the steps below to delete registered fingerprints.

1   From the Settings screen, click **Security and privacy,** go to **Biometrics,** and select **Fingerprints**.

2   Unlock the screen by using your current method of unlocking the screen.

3   Select a fingerprint to delete and click **Remove**.

Extend Unlock

This feature (previously called Smart Lock) allows you to configure your Galaxy A15 5G to unlock itself and stay unlocked when trusted locations or devices are detected.

For example, if you have set your home or office as a trusted location, whenever you get home or to your office, your device will detect the location and automatically unlock itself.

From the **Settings** screen, click **Lock screen** → **Extend Unlock** and follow the on-screen instructions to finish the setup.

NOTE:

- You will be able to use this feature only after you have set a screen lock method.
- If you have not used your device for at least four hours or when you turn it on, you must have to unlock the screen by using the pattern, PIN, or password you set.

Secure Folder

Secure Folder helps you to secure your private content and apps, such as pictures and contacts, from being accessible to others even when your phone is unlocked.

CAUTION:

Secure Folder is a distinct, secured storage area. You cannot transfer the data in Secure Folder to other devices by means of unauthorized sharing methods, such as USB or Wi-Fi Direct. Any attempt to personalize the operating system or modifying software will cause Secure Folder to be automatically locked and inaccessible. Before saving data in Secure Folder, be sure you have a backup copy of the data in another secure location.

How to Set up Secure Folder

1. Open the **Settings** app and click **Security and privacy** > **More security settings** > **Secure Folder**.
2. Complete the setup by following the on-screen instructions.

    Tap **Turn on** when a pop-up window requesting you to reset the Secure Folder lock type using your Samsung account appears. Using your Samsung account, you can reset the lock type if you've forgotten it. You won't be able to reset the lock type if you don't activate this feature after you forget it.

Once the process is complete, the Secure Folder screen will display and the Secure Folder app icon (◉) will be added to the Apps screen.

To change the name or icon color of Secure Folder, click ⋮ and go to **Customize**.

NOTE:
- To open the **Secure Folder** app, you'll have to unlock the app using your preset lock technique.

Setting an auto lock condition for Secure Folder

1. Open the **Secure Folder** app and click ⋮ → **Settings** → **Auto lock Secure Folder**.
2. Choose a lock option.

NOTE: You can manually lock your Secure Folder by clicking ⋮ and selecting **Lock and exit**.

How to Move content to Secure Folder

Transfer content, such as pictures and videos, to Secure Folder. The following steps are a guide to the process of moving an image from the default storage to Secure Folder.

1. Start the **Secure Folder** app and click ⋮ → **Add files**.

2. Click **Images**, tick images to move, and then click **Done**.

3. Click **Move**.

   The ticked items will be deleted from the original folder and moved to Secure Folder. To copy items, click **Copy**.

NOTE: The method for moving content may not be the same, depending on the content type.

Moving content from Secure Folder

Transfer files from the Secure Folder to the appropriate app in the default storage location. The following steps will show you how to transfer a picture from the Secure Folder to the default storage location.

1. Launch the **Secure Folder** app and navigate to the **Gallery** menu option.

2. Select the image to move, tap ⋮ and then hit the button labeled "**Move out of Secure Folder**."

3. The objects that you have chosen will have their default storage location changed to the **Gallery** folder.

Adding apps

Add an app to use in Secure Folder.

1. Open the **Secure Folder** app and tap the **Add** icon ✚.

2   Choose one or more apps installed on your phone and tap **Add**.

Removing apps from Secure Folder

Tap and hold an app to delete, and then tap **Uninstall**.

Adding accounts

Add any of your accounts, like Samsung and Google accounts, or other accounts, to sync with the apps in Secure Folder.

1   Launch the **Secure Folder** app and click ⋮ → **Settings** → **Manage accounts** → **Add account**.

2   Choose an account service.

3   Complete the account setup by following the on-screen instructions.

Hiding Secure Folder

You will be able to hide the Secure Folder shortcut, if you like, from the Apps screen.

Launch the **Secure Folder** app, tap ⋮→**Settings**, and then click **Add Secure Folder to Apps screen** and turn off the switch.

Alternatively, open the notification panel, swipe down, and then click 🔒 (**Secure Folder**) to deactivate the feature.

If you can't find it there, tap the **Add** button and drag it over to include it.

If you want the Secure Folder to be visible again, start the **Settings** app, click **Security and privacy** > **Biometrics** > **Secure Folder**, and then click the **Add Secure folder to Apps screen** switch to activate it.

Uninstalling Secure Folder

If you wish to, you can uninstall Secure Folder, including the content and apps in it any time.

Open the **Secure Folder** app and click the **More options** tab ⋮. From there, go to **Setting** > **More settings,** and tap **Uninstall**.

If you want to back up your files before uninstalling Secure Folder, tick **Move media files out of Secure Folder** and select the **Uninstall** option. To access the backed-up data from Secure Folder, open the **My Files** app and click **Internal storage,** then go to **Download,** and then **Secure Folder**.

NOTE: Notes saved in **Samsung Notes** are not going to have a backup.

Secure Wi-Fi

Secure Wi-Fi is a service that secures your Wi-Fi network connection. It encrypts data by using Wi-Fi networks and disables tracking apps and websites in a way that you can use Wi-Fi networks securely.

For example, when using an unsecure Wi-Fi network in public places, such as cafes or airports, Secure Wi-Fi is automatically activated in a manner that no one will be able to hack your login information or watch your activity in apps and websites.

From the **Settings** menu, select **Security and privacy**, select **More Security settings,** then select **Secure Wi-Fi** and follow the on-screen instructions to complete the setup.

When you activate the Secure Wi-Fi, the Wi-Fi icon will be displayed on the status bar.

NOTE:
- Using this feature may result in a decreased Wi-Fi network speed.
- This feature may not be available depending on the Wi-Fi network, service provider, or model.

How to select the apps to protect with Secure Wi-Fi

You can select the apps you want to protect using Secure Wi-Fi to safely protect data, such as your password or your activity in apps, from being accessed by anyone else.

Go to **Settings**, click **Security and privacy** > **More security settings** > **Secure Wi-Fi**. Then tap the **More options** tab (⋮) on the top right corner) and go to **Settings** > **Protected apps** and click the switches next to the apps you want to protect using Secure Wi-Fi.

NOTE: Some apps may not support this feature.

How to buy a protection plan

There's a free protection plan for Wi-Fi networks every month for you. But you can as well buy paid protection plans and get unlimited bandwidth protection for a restricted time.

1. From the Settings screen, click **Security and privacy** > **More security settings** > **Secure Wi-Fi**.
2. Tap **Protection plan** and **Upgrade** options from their respective menus, and then choose the plan you want.

    NOTE: For some kind of protection plans, you can transfer the protection plan to another device signed in to your Samsung account.

3. Complete the purchase by following the on-screen instructions.

Samsung Pass

When you register your biometric data to Samsung Pass, you can easily verify your identity when using services which require you to login or provide personal information.

NOTE:

- Some websites may not support this feature, unless for those you access via the **Samsung Internet** app.
- Registered biometric data is saved to your device alone. It is not synced with other devices or servers.

How to register Samsung Pass

Before using Samsung Pass, you must register your biometric data to Samsung Pass.

On the Settings screen, click **Security and privacy**, select **More security settings,** and then select **Samsung Pass**. Finish the setup by following the on-screen instructions.

Verifying the Samsung account password

You can use your registered biometric data to confirm your identity instead of using your Samsung account password wherever necessary, e.g. when you purchase content from **Galaxy Store**.

When you open the Samsung Pass main screen, click the **More options** tab ⋮, select **Settings** from the available options, select **Account and syncing** from the next screen, and then tap the **Verify with Samsung Pass** switch to activate it.

Using Samsung Pass to sign in to websites.

Samsung Pass can be used to easily sign in to websites that support ID and password autofill.

1 On the sign-in page of the website, input your ID and password, and then click the website's sign-in button.

2 When a pop-up window asking whether you want to save the sign-in information displays, tick the option that says, "**Sign in with Samsung Pass**" and click **Remember**.

Using Samsung Pass to sign in to apps.

Just like signing in to websites with Samsung Pass, you can also easily sign in to apps that support ID and password autofill using Samsung Pass. Follow these two simple steps:

1 On the sign-in page of the app, input your ID and password, and then click the app's sign-in button.

2. When a pop-up window asking whether you want to save the sign-in information displays, click the **Save** option.

How to sign in with Passkeys

You can use a passkey saved in Samsung Pass to login in to apps or websites that accept it instead of using your ID and password.

1. Create a passkey in the app or website you're using. The process for creating a passkey may vary based on the app or website.
2. When prompted to save your passkey, select **Samsung Pass**.
3. To save the passkey, simply follow the on-screen instructions.

   You can now sign in using the passkey saved in Samsung Pass.

Managing sign-in information

Look the list of websites and apps you have set to use Samsung Pass and manage information about your sign-in.

1. From the Samsung Pass main screen, click **Apps/Websites,** and choose a website or app from the list.

2   Click **Edit** and change your ID, password, and the website's or app's name.

To delete your sign-in information, click the **Delete** button.

Using Samsung Pass with websites and apps

If you're using websites or apps that support Samsung Pass, you can easily sign in with Samsung Pass.

To know if a website and app supports Samsung Pass, on the Samsung Pass main screen, click ⋮ and select **Partners**. If there are no websites or apps that support Samsung Pass, you will not see **Partners**.

How to fill your personal information automatically

Your Samsung Pass can be used to easily enter your personal information, such as your address or payment card information, on apps that support autofill.

1   On the Samsung Pass main screen, choose an option under **Private info**.

2   Enter the information and click **Save**.

You can now use the biometric data you registered to Samsung Pass when entering the personal information automatically on apps that support this feature.

Deleting your Samsung Pass data

You can be able delete your biometric data, sign-in information, and app data registered to Samsung Pass.

From the Samsung Pass main screen, tap ⋮ → **Settings**, go to **Devices using Samsung Pass**, tap ⋮, and then select **Leave Samsung Pass**.

NOTE:

- Your Samsung account will remain active.
- The Samsung Pass data on other devices signed in to your Samsung account will also be deleted.

Chapter Four

GETTING USED TO YOUR PHONE'S FEATURES AND FUNCTIONS

Understanding the screen

Controlling the touch screen

Tapping
Tap the screen.

Tapping and holding
Tap and hold the screen for approximately 2 seconds.

Dragging
Tap and hold an item and drag it to the target position.

Double-tapping
Double-tap the screen.

Swiping
Swipe upwards, downwards, to the left, or to the right.

Spreading and pinching
Spread two fingers apart or pinch on the screen.

CAUTION:

- Never allow the touch screen to come into contact with other electrical devices. Electrostatic discharges can make the touch screen to malfunction.

- To avoid damaging the touch screen, do not tap it with anything sharp object, or apply any excessive pressure to it with your fingertips.
- It is recommended not to use fixed graphics on part or all the touch screen for prolonged periods as this may cause afterimages (screen burn-in) or ghosting.

NOTE:

The device may not be able to identify touch inputs close to the edges of the screen, which are not within the touch input area.

Navigation bar (soft buttons)

Any time you turn on the screen, the soft buttons will display on the navigation bar at the bottom of the screen. By default, the soft buttons are configured to the **Recents** button, **Home** button, and **Back** button from left to right respectively. The functions of the buttons can change depending on the app currently being used or operating environment. (See *Soft buttons and their functions* in Chapter One for more information).

Hiding the navigation bar

Hiding the navigation bar enables you to view files or use apps on a wider screen.

From the **Settings** app, tap **Display**, go to **Navigation bar**, and then tap **Swipe gestures** under **Navigation type**. The navigation bar will be hidden, and the gesture hints will show up. Tap **More options** and select the one you prefer from the displayed options.

Swipe from bottom   Swipe from sides and bottom

If you like to hide the gesture hints at the bottom of the screen, tap the **Gesture hints** switch to deactivate it.

Home screen and Apps screen

The Home screen is the starting point from where you can access all the features of your device. It shows widgets, shortcuts to apps, and much more.

The Apps screen displays icons for all apps installed on your device.

How to switch quickly between Home and Apps screens

To open the Apps screen, swipe the Home screen upwards.

To return to the Home screen, swipe the Apps screen upwards or downwards; or instead, tap the Home button or the Back button.

Home screen (Favourite apps) / *Apps screen* (Finder)

If the Apps button has been added on the Home screen, you can open the Apps screen simply by tapping the button. To add it, follow the simple steps:

1. On the Home screen, tap and hold an empty area.

2. Tap **Settings**

3. Activate the **Show Apps screen button on Home screen** by tapping the switch.

The Apps button is straightaway added at the bottom of the Home screen.

— Apps button

How to edit the Home screen

From the Home screen, **tap and hold an empty space, or pinch your fingers together to view the editing options**. Here, you can set the wallpaper; add widgets; and add, delete, or rearrange Home screen panels.

- To add panels, swipe to the left, and then tap the **Add** button ✚.

- To move panels, tap and hold a panel preview, then drag it to a new location.

- To delete panels, tap the bin icon 🗑 on the panel.

- **Wallpapers and style**: You can change the wallpaper settings for the Home screen and the locked screen.

- **Themes**: You can change the device's theme. Note that visual elements of interface, such as colors, icons, and wallpapers, will change according to the selected theme.
- **Widgets**: These are small apps that launch specific app functions to give information and convenient access on your Home screen. Select a widget and tap **Add**. The widget will be added on the Home screen accordingly.
- **Settings**: Organize settings for the Home screen, such as the screen layout.

Displaying all apps on the Home screen

If you don't want to use a separate Apps screen, you can set the device to display all your apps on the Home screen. On the Home screen, just tap and hold an empty area, and then tap **Settings** > **Home screen layout** > **Home screen only** > **Apply**.

With that, you'll be able to access all your apps by swiping to the left on the Home screen.

Launching Finder

Quickly search for content on the device.

1. On the Apps screen, tap **Search**. Otherwise, open the notification panel and swipe downwards, then tap Q.
2. Type in a keyword. All the apps and content on your device will be searched.

You can search for more content by taping Q on the keyboard.

Moving items

1. Tap and hold an item
2. Drag it to a new location.
3. Drag it to the side of the screen if you want to move the item to another panel.

Adding a shortcut to an app on the Home screen:

1. Tap and hold an item on the Apps screen
2. Tap **Add to Home**.

If you like, you can also move frequently used apps to the shortcuts area at the bottom of the Home screen.

Creating folders

Create folders and collect related apps to quickly access and launch apps.

1. On the Home screen or the Apps screen, tap and hold an app

2. Drag the selected app over another app. A new folder comprising the selected apps will be created. 3. Tap **Folder name** and input a folder name.

- **Adding more apps**

    Simply tap ✚ on the folder. Select the apps to add by ticking them and tap **Done**. Alternately, just drag the app you want to add to the folder.

- **Moving apps from a folder**

    Tap and hold an app if you want to drag it to a new location.

- **Deleting a folder**

    Tap and hold a folder, and then tap the **Delete folder**. Note that only the folder will be deleted. The apps in the folder will be relocated to the Apps screen.

Edge panel

The Edge panel enables you to quickly access your favorite apps and features.

Pull the Edge panel handle towards the center of the screen.

If the Edge panel handle is not visible on the screen, go to the **Settings** app, tap **Display**, and then tap the **Edge panels** switch to activate.

Lock screen

Anytime you press the Side button, the screen turns off and locks. The screen will also turn off and automatically lock if the phone is idle for a given period.

To unlock the screen, turn it on and swipe in any direction of the screen.

If the screen is off, turn it on by pressing the Side button or you double-click the screen instead.

Changing the screen lock method

To change how the screen locks, open the **Settings** app, tap **Lock screen** > **Screen lock type**, and then choose a method.

Setting a pattern, PIN, password, or your biometric data for the screen lock method protects your personal information by preventing others from having unauthorized access to your device. After setting the screen lock method, the device will require an unlock code anytime you want to unlock it.

NOTE: If you want your device to do a factory data reset if you enter the unlock code wrong too many times in a row and reach the maximum number of attempts, open the **Settings** app, click **Lock screen** > **Secure lock settings**, unlock the screen using the preset screen lock method, and then tap the **Auto factory reset** switch to turn it on.

Indicator icons

Indicator icons will show on the status bar at the top of the screen. The icons shown in the table below are most commonly in use:

Icon	Meaning
⊘	No signal
.ıll	Signal strength
ᴿ.ıll	Roaming (outside of normal service area)
G ↓↑	GPRS network connected
E ↓↑	EDGE network connected
3G ↓↑	UMTS network connected
H ↓↑	HSDPA network connected
H+ ↓↑	HSPA+ network connected
4G ↓↑ / LTE ↓↑	LTE network connected
5G ↓↑	5G network connected
5G ↓↑	Connected to LTE network with the 5G network
📶	Wi-Fi connected
✷	Bluetooth feature activated
◉	Location services being used
☏	Call in progress
☏	Missed call
💬	New text or multimedia message
⏰	Alarm activated

🔇 / 📳	Mute mode / Vibration mode
✈	Flight mode activated
⚠	Error occurred or caution required
/ 🔋 🪫	Battery charging / Battery power level

NOTE:

- The status bar may not show at the top of the screen in some apps. To show the status bar, drag down from the top of the screen.

- Some indicator icons show only when you open the notification panel.

- The indicator icons may show separately based on the service provider or model.

Notification panel

Anytime you receive new notifications, indicator icons will show on the status bar. To see additional information about the icons, open the notification panel and view the details.

Quick settings — Open **Settings**.

Control connected nearby devices and SmartThings devices and scenes.

Adjust the brightness of the display.

Check the notification details and perform various actions.

Control media on your phone and connected nearby devices.

Access the notification settings.

Clear all notifications.

Drag the status bar downwards to open the notification panel, and swipe upwards on the screen to close it.

The following functions on the notification panel commonly used:

Using quick setting buttons

Simply swipe downwards on the notification panel or swipe down twice from the top of the screen on the Home screen to open the Quick settings panel. Tap any button to activate its specific features. Touch and hold any button or simply tap its name to get additional settings. Tap ✏ at the top of the screen and select **Edit** to make edits to any button.

Quick settings buttons

Adjust screen brightness

63

Controlling media playback

With the Media feature, you can take total control of your music or video playback. You can also continue playback on another device.

1. Open the notification panel and click **Media output**.
2. Tap the icons on the controller to take charge and control the playback.
3. To continue the playback on another device, touch 🕲 and pick the device you want.

Controlling nearby devices

Launch swiftly and be in control of nearby connected devices and frequently used SmartThings devices and scenes on the notification panel.

1. Open the notification panel on your phone and tap **Device control**.

   Nearby connected devices and SmartThings devices and scenes will show up.

2. Select a nearby device or a SmartThings device to control it or select a scene to launch it.

Chapter Five

COMMUNICATIONS

The Phone app

The Phone app is used to make/receive voice and video calls.

NOTE:

- If the part around the rear camera is covered, unwanted noises may be experienced during a call.
- Remove any accessories like screen protector and stickers close to the back camera.

Making calls

1. Open the **Phone** app and tap **Keypad**.

2. Enter a phone number.

3. Tap 🔵 to make a voice call or tap 📹 or 📷 if you want to make a video call.

Making calls from call logs or contacts list

Open the **Phone** app, tap **Recents** or **Contacts**, and then swipe to the right on a contact or a phone number to make a call.

If this feature is not on, tap ⋮ → **Settings** → **Other call settings**, followed by a tap on **Swipe to call or text** switch to activate it.

How to use speed dial

To assign a number to speed dial, open the **Phone** app, tap **Keypad** or **Contacts**, tap the **More options** tab ⋮ and select **Speed dial numbers**, select a speed dial number, and then add a phone number.

To make a call, simply click and hold a speed dial number on the keypad. For speed dial numbers from 10 upwards, click the first digit(s) of the number, and then tap and hold the last digit.

For example, if you set the number 234 as a speed dial number, tap 2, tap 3, and then press and hold 4.

Making an international call

1 Open the **Phone** app and click **Keypad**.
2 Touch and hold **0** until it changes to the plus (+) sign.

3   Type in the country code, area code, and phone number, and then tap 🕾.

Receiving calls

How to answer a call

When you have an incoming call, drag 🕾 outside the large circle to receive the call.

How to reject a call

When you have an incoming call, drag 🕾 outside the large circle to reject the call.

If you wish to send a message when rejecting an incoming call, drag the **Send message** bar upwards and choose a message to send.

To create different rejection messages, open the **Phone** app, tap ⋮ → **Settings** → **Quick decline messages**, type a message, and then tap ＋.

Blocking phone numbers

Block calls coming through from numbers added to your block list.

1   Open the **Phone** app and tap ⋮ → **Settings** → **Block numbers**.

2 Select the contacts or phone numbers you want to block from **Recents** or **Contacts** and save them in the block numbers list. To manually enter a number, tap **Add phone number**, type in a phone number, and then tap ✚.

When blocked numbers attempt to reach you, you will not receive notifications. You will find the calls in the call log.

NOTE:

If you like to block incoming calls from people who hide their caller ID, just tap the **Block unknown/private numbers** switch to activate the feature.

Things you can do during a call.

The following options are available to you while making a call with your phone:

- **Add call**: you can dial a second call while making a call. The first call will be placed on hold. When you end the second call, the first call will resume.
- **Video call**: You can switch to a video call from a voice call.
- **Hold call**: Place a call on hold.
- **Bluetooth**: Shift to a Bluetooth headset if it is connected to the device.

- **Speaker**: You may wish to activate or deactivate the speakerphone. When you are using the speakerphone, do not keep the device close to your ears.
- **Mute**: When you turn off the microphone, the other party will not be able to hear you.
- **Keypad/Hide**: Open or close keypad.
- Tap ⬤ to end the current call.
- Tap ☏ to switch to a voice call from a video call.
- **Camera**: During a video call, if you turn off the camera, the other party cannot see you.
- **Switch**: During a video call, you can switch between the front and back cameras.
- Select ⬤ to set your phone to automatically adjust the angle and zoom by identifying and tracking individuals during a video call.
- Tap ⬤ to lock the screen when making a video call.
- Select ⬤ to change the screen ration while making a video call.
- **Effects**: Use this feature to apply different effects during a video call.

NOTE: Some features may be restricted depending on the service provider or model.

The Contacts app

This app enables you to create new contacts or manage contacts on your phone.

How to save contacts to your Galaxy A15 5G

Create a new contact.

1. Open the **Contacts** app and tap ✛.
2. Pick a storage location.
3. Input contact information and tap **Save**.

Import contacts from other sources.

You may also like to add contacts by importing them from other storage media to your device.

1. Open the **Contacts** app and click the **Menu** tab ☰, select **Manage contacts**, then tap **Import contacts**.
2. Follow the instructions that display on the screen to import contacts.

Syncing contacts with your web accounts

You can set your device contacts to synchronize with online contacts saved in your web accounts, such as your Samsung account or Google account. Just follow the simple steps outlined below:

1 Open the **Settings** app, tap **Accounts and backup**, then tap **Manage accounts** and choose the account to sync with.

2 Tap **Sync account** and tap the **Contacts** switch to get it activated.

How to find contacts on your phone

Open the **Contacts** app. Tap the **Search** icon 🔍 at the top of the contacts menu and type in any keyword related to the contact, e.g. name.

Tap the contact you want, and then take an action from the following options:

- 📞 : Make a voice call.
- 📹 / 📷 : Make a video call.
- 💬 : Compose a message.
- ✉ : Compose an email.

Deleting contacts

1 When you open the **Contacts** app, tap on the **More options** tab, ⋮ and select **Edit**.

2 Select the contacts you wish to delete, and tap **Delete**.

To delete contacts one by one, tap a contact from the contacts menu and tap **More → Delete**.

Sharing contacts

You can your share contacts with others by using several sharing options:

1 When you open the **Contacts** app, tap on the **More options** tab, ⋮ and select **Edit**.
2 Select the contacts you want and tap the **Share** button.
3 Choose a method to share with.

Creating groups

If you like to add groups, such as family or friends, and manage contacts by group, follow these steps:

1 Open the **Contacts** app and tap the **Menu** tab ≡, then select **Groups,** and then **Create group**.
2 Follow the on-screen directives to create a group.

How to merge duplicate contacts

If you have duplicated contacts in your list, merge them into one to update your contacts list.

1 Open the **Contacts** app and tap ≡ →**Manage contacts** → **Merge contacts**.
2 Tick contacts and tap **Merge**.

The Messages app

This is app lets you send and view messages by conversation.

You may need to pay additional charges for sending or receiving messages while roaming.

How to enter text

Keyboard layout

A keyboard displays automatically when you enter text.

```
Additional keyboard functions ──┐                ┌── View more keyboard functions.
Enter uppercase. For all caps, tap it ──┐        ┌── Delete a preceding character.
                        twice.
            Enter symbols. ──┐                   ┌── Break to the next line.
                                                 └── Enter a space.
```

NOTE: Not all languages support Text entry. To enter text, you must first change the input language to one that is supported.

Changing the input language

To change language, tap ⚙ the settings cog, then tap **Languages and types** > **Manage input languages** and pick the languages to use. When you select two or more languages, you can switch from one input language to another by swiping to the left or right on the space key.

Changing the keyboard

To change the keyboard, open the navigation bar and tap ⌨ the keyboard icon.

To change the keyboard type, tap the settings cog, ⚙ > **Languages and types**, pick a language, and then select the keyboard type you wish to use.

NOTE:

- If the keyboard button (⌨) does not show on the navigation bar, start the **Settings** app, click **General management** > **Keyboard list and default**, and then click **Keyboard button on navigation bar** switch to activate the feature.

- On a **3 x 4** keyboard, a key comprises of three or four characters. To input a character, click the corresponding key repeatedly until the desired character appears.

Copying and pasting

1. Tap and hold over the text you want to copy.
2. Drag ● ● to the extent you wish to highlight the desired text, or tap **Select all** to select all text.
3. Click **Copy** or **Cut**.

    The text you have highlighted will be copied to the clipboard.

4   Touch and hold the area where the text is to be pasted and click **Paste** to insert the copied text.

To paste text that has already been copied, just tap **Clipboard,** and select the given text.

Additional keyboard functions

- ☺ : Enter stickers. You can also input your emoji stickers that look like you. Check out *Using your emoji stickers in chats* for more details.
- 🈁 : Attach animated GIFs.
- 🎤 : Enter text by voice.
- ⚙ : Change the keyboard settings.
- 🅰 : Translate text and enter it in.
- 📋 : Add an item from the clipboard.
- 📱 : Switch to one-handed mode.
- ⌨ : Change the keyboard mode.
- 🔤 : Recognize text from documents or images and insert it.
- ＋ : Edit the keyboard function list.
- Tap the ellipsis ••• to use more keyboard functions.

Sending messages

1. Open the **Messages** app and tap ⓐ.
2. Add recipients and enter a message.

    If you like to record and send a voice message, tap and hold ᴴᴵᴴ, say your message, and then release your finger from the icon. The recording icon will only appear when the message input field is empty.

3. Tap 🕗 to send the message.

```
Recipient ——— [ New conversation ]         Enter recipients.

Enter a message. ———                        Enter stickers.

Attach files. ———                           Send the message.
```

Viewing messages

1. Open the **Messages** app and tap **Conversations**.
2. On the message menu, pick a contact or a phone number.

    - If you're replying to the message, tap the message input field, enter a message, and then tap send [🕗].

- To adjust the font size, drag two fingers apart or pinch on the screen.

Sorting messages

You can sort messages by category and manage them without stress.

Open the **Messages** app and tap **Conversations** and tap the plus sign (✛) to add category.

If the category option does not show, tap ⋮ > **Settings** and tap the **Conversations categories** switch for it to be activated.

Deleting messages

Just tap and hold a message to delete, then tap **Delete**.

Changing message settings

Mount the **Messages** app, tap ⋮ > **Settings**. Here, you can also block unwanted messages, change notification settings, and so on.

Internet

Browse the Internet to search for information and bookmark your favorite web pages to access them.

1 Launch the **Internet** app.
2 Type in the web address or a keyword, and then tap **Go**.

For you to view the toolbars, just drag your finger downwards a little on the screen.

If you want to switch between tabs swiftly, swipe to the left or right on the address field.

Bookmark the current webpage.

Refresh the current webpage.

View you bookmarks.

Open the homepage.

Manage taps. / User secret mode.

Move between pages.

More options

Using secret mode

You can prevent others from viewing your search history, browsing history, bookmarks, and saved pages by setting a password for secret mode.

1 Touch ▭→**Turn on Secret mode**.
2 Touch the **Lock Secret mode** switch to activate it, touch **Start**, and then set a password for secret mode.
   In secret mode, the device will normally change the color of the toolbars. Anytime you want to deactivate secret mode, touch ▭ → **Turn off Secret mode**.

NOTE: In secret mode, some features, such as screen capture may not be available.

Chapter Six

THE CAMERA AND GALLERY APPS

Camera

Capture pictures and record videos with various modes and settings.

Take note of the following camera etiquette

- Never take pictures or record videos of other people unless they have permitted you to do so.
- Do not take pictures or record videos in places where it is legally forbidden.
- Avoid taking pictures or recording videos in places where your action may result in violation of other people's privacy.

How to take pictures with your phone

1. Open the **Camera** app.

   You can also launch the app by pressing the Side key twice quickly or by dragging the camera icon (󰄀) to the left on the locked screen.

2. Touch the image on the preview screen where you want the camera to focus.

- To adjust the brightness of pictures, pull the adjustment bar that displays above or below the circular frame.

3. Tap ◯ to take a picture.

- To alter the shooting mode, pull the shooting modes list to the left or right, or swipe either to the left or right on the preview screen.

Camera settings — Options for current shooting mode

Zoom

Preview thumbnail

Take a picture.

Shooting modes list

Switch between the front and rear cameras.

NOTE:

- Some features of the camera are absent when you launch the **Camera** app from the locked screen or when the screen is turned off if your device has its screen lock method set.

- The camera automatically shuts off when it's not in use.
- Some methods may be absent depending on the service provider or model.
- The preview screen may differ based on the shooting mode and the type of camera being used.
- High resolution and high zoom ratio decrease the clarity of pictures and videos when taken from a close range. Therefore, maintain a good distance when taking pictures or videos.
- If you take pictures and they appear blurry, clean the camera lens and try taking again.
- Ensure that the lens is never damaged or contaminated. Or else, the device may not work well in some modes requiring high resolutions.
- Your device's camera possesses a wide-angle lens. Slight alteration may occur in wide-angle pictures or videos and does not imply device performance problems.
- The highest capacity for video recording may differ depending on the resolution.
- If the device is exposed to sudden changes in air temperature, the camera may fog up or form condensation

because of the difference in temperature outside and inside the camera cover. Take caution to avoid such conditions when planning to use the camera. If fogging occurs, allow the camera to dry naturally at room temperature before taking pictures or recording videos, otherwise results may look blurry.

How to use the zoom features on your Galaxy A15 5G

To zoom in or out on an image, tap the zoom icon (**.5x/1x/2x**) displayed on the preview screen and make your selection, or simply drag it to the left or right to zoom in or out respectively.

Alternatively, you can select your desired zoom level from the zoom level list displayed under the zoom icon when you tap it.

Furthermore, you can pinch on the screen to zoom out or spread two fingers apart on the screen to zoom in, if you want to be more precise.

Zoom

Zoom level list

NOTE:

- **.5x**: The Ultra-wide camera allows you to take wide-angle pictures or record wide-angle videos of things such as landscapes.
- **1x**: The wide-angle camera allows you to take basic pictures or record normal simple videos.
- **2x**: The telephoto camera enables you to take pictures or record videos by increasing the subject size.
- You can only make use of the zoom features when using the rear camera.

Locking the focus (AF) and exposure (AE)

You can lock the focus or exposure on a selected portion to inhibit the camera from automatically adjusting based on changes to the subjects or light sources.

Tap and hold the portion to focus, the AF/AE frame will display on the portion and the focus and exposure setting will be locked. The setting will remain locked even after you take a picture.

NOTE: The availability of this feature is subject to the shooting mode.

How to use the camera button

- Touch and hold the camera button to record a video.

- If you like to take burst shots, simply swipe the camera button to the edge of the screen and hold it.
- Create GIFs by tapping the **Settings** icon ✦ on the preview screen and selecting the option "**Swipe Shutter button to**", and then "**Create GIF**".
- If you've added another camera button, you can move it anywhere on the screen and take pictures more handily. On the preview screen, touch ✦ → **Shooting methods** and touch the **Floating Shutter button** switch to activate it.

Options for current shooting mode

On the preview screen, make use of the following options:

- ⚡ : To activate or deactivate the flash.
- ⏲ : Choose how long to delay before the camera automatically takes a picture.
- 3:4 : Choose an aspect ratio and resolution for your pictures.
- 12M : Select a desired resolution for taking photos.
- ▣ : To activate or deactivate the motion photo feature. If this feature is activated, a video clip will

also be taken from a few seconds before tapping the camera button.

- 🏃 : To activate or deactivate the super steady feature to calm a video.

- AUTO : To pick a frame rate.

- ⏱ : Change the recording time for hyperlapse videos.

- 9:16 : Choose an aspect ratio for videos.

- FHD 30 : Choose a resolution for videos.

- ◈ : To apply any filter effect or beauty effects.

- ◎ : To choose a metering method. This controls how light values are calculated. ◎**Centre-weighted** makes use of the light in the center portion of the shot to determine the exposure of the shot. (o) **Spot metering** makes use of the light in a concentrated center portion of the shot to determine the exposure of the shot. (o) **Matrix metering** takes the average the entire scene.

- ◯ : In **FOOD** mode, instructing to focus on a subject within the circular frame and blur the image outside the frame.

- ⊚ : Instructing to regulate the color tone.

- 🌡 : Adjust the color temperature in **FOOD** mode

NOTE: The options available may differ according to the model or shooting mode.

How to use the Photo mode on Galaxy A15 5G

The camera regulates the shooting options automatically based on the immediate surroundings to capture pictures easily.

From the shooting modes menu, tap **PHOTO** and tap ◯ to take a picture.

Taking high-resolution pictures

Take high-resolution pictures following these simple steps: In the shooting options, tap **12M**, then choose the resolution you want to use and take a picture.

NOTE: If this feature has not been activated, tap ⚙ on the preview screen and tap the **Scene optimizer** switch to activate it.

How to take good selfies with your Galaxy A15 phone

You can take self-portraits with the front camera of your smartphone.

1. On the preview screen, swipe upwards or downwards, or click ⬤ to switch to the front camera for self-portraits.

2. Face the front camera lens.

If you want to take self-portraits with a wide-angle shot of the landscape or people, click 🔘.

3. Click ⭕ to take a picture.

How to Apply filter and beauty effects to your shots

You can choose a filter effect and alter facial features, such as your skin tone or face shape, before taking a picture.

1. On the preview screen, click 🔶.

2. Choose effects and take a picture.

You can tap ➕ to download filters from the **Galaxy Store**, or if you like, you can use the **My filters style** to create your own filter by using an image with a color tone you love from the **Gallery app**.

Video mode

The camera will adjust the shooting options automatically in relation on the surroundings to record videos easily.

1 On the shooting modes menu, click **VIDEO** and click ⦿ to record a video.
- To switch from the front to the rear camera and vice versa while recording, swipe upwards or downwards on the preview screen or click ◉
- To snap an image from the video while recording, press the Capture button ◯ on the screen.

2 Tap the **Stop button** ■ to stop recording the video.

Portrait mode

The camera enables you to take shots where the background is blurred, and the subject stands out clearly.

1 Tap **PORTRAIT** from the shooting modes menu.

2 Tap ◉ and move the background blur adjustment bar to adjust the blur level.

3 As soon as you see **Ready** appear on the preview screen, tap the capture button ◯ to take a picture.

Background blur adjustment bar

NOTE:

- This feature is best used in a place with sufficient light.
- The background blur may be poorly applied due to the following conditions:

— The device or the subject is moving.

— The subject is thin or transparent.

— The subject has a similar color to the background.

— The subject or background is plain.

Fun mode

Take a picture with numerous effects.

1. On the shooting modes list, click **FUN**.
2. To choose a different effect, slide the camera button to the left or right.

3. Tap on the effect button to take a photo or touch and hold the effect button to record a video.

Pro mode

Capture pictures as you manually adjust different shooting options, such as exposure value and ISO value.

From the shooting modes menu, click **MORE→PRO**. Choose options and customize the settings, and then tap ⭕ to take a picture.

Available options

⭕ : Reset the settings.

ISO : Choose an ISO value. This regulates camera light sensitivity. Smaller ISO values are used for stationary or well luminous objects. Higher values are used for fast-moving objects or objects with poor illumination. Nevertheless, higher ISO settings can cause noise in pictures or videos.

SPEED: Regulate the shutter speed. A slow shutter speed lets more light in, so the picture becomes brighter. This is perfect for pictures or videos of scenery, or pictures taken at night. A fast shutter speed lets less light in. This is perfect for capturing pictures of fast-moving subjects.

•

EV : Change the exposure value. This controls how much light the camera's sensor receives. For low-light occasions, use a higher exposure.

FOCUS: Change the focus mode. Move the adjustment bar towards or to adjust the focus by yourself to satisfaction.

WB : Select a suitable white balance, to make your images have a true-to-life color range. You can also set the color temperature.

Separating the focus area and the exposure area

It is possible to separate the focus area and the exposure area.

Click and hold the preview screen. The AF/AE frame will display on the screen. Move the frame to the place where you want to separate the focus area and the exposure area.

Night mode

Take a picture in low-light environment, without using the flash. When you use a tripod, you can get better results.

1   From the shooting modes menu, tap **MORE→NIGHT**.

2   Click ◯ and hold your device stable until shooting is complete.

Food mode

You can capture pictures of food with more lively colors.

1. From the shooting modes menu, click **MORE→FOOD**.

2. Touch the screen and pull the circular frame over the area to highlight.

    The area outside the circular frame will be hazy.

    To resize the circular frame, move a corner of the frame.

3. Tap 🌡 and move the adjustment bar to adjust the color tone.

4. Click ◯ to take a picture.

Panorama mode

You can take a series of pictures and then stitch them together to create a wide scene using the panorama mode.

1. From the shooting modes menu, click **MORE** → **PANORAMA**.

2. Click ◯ and move the device slowly in one direction. Retain the image inside the frame on the camera's viewfinder. If the preview image is not inside the guide frame or you don't move the device, the device will automatically cease to take pictures.

3. Click ◯ to stop taking pictures.

NOTE: It's not advisable taking pictures of indistinct backgrounds, like an empty sky or a plain wall.

Macro mode

Allows you to take pictures of subjects at close range.

From the shooting modes menu, click **MORE** → **MACRO**.

Slow motion mode

Record a video to view it in slow motion. You can stipulate segments of your videos to be played in slow motion.

1. From the shooting modes menu, tap **MORE→SLOW MOTION** and tap ⦿ to record a video.

2. When you are done recording, tap ⦿ to stop.

3. On the preview screen, click the preview thumbnail and click **Play slow motion video**.

The fast segment of the video will be set as a slow-motion segment and the video will start playing. Up to two slow motion segments will be created according to the video.

To edit the slow-motion segment, tap the pencil icon ⌀ and move the segment editing bar to the left or right.

Super slow-motion section — Section editing bar — End bracket — Start bracket

Hyperlapse mode

This feature enables you to record scenes, like passing people or cars, and view them as fast-motion videos.

1. On the shooting modes menu, click **MORE** → **HYPERLAPSE**.
2. Tap **AUTO** and pick a frame rate option.

    If you set the frame rate to **AUTO**, the device will automatically regulate the frame rate depending on the changing rate of the scene.

3. Tap the start button ⦿ to begin the recording.

4. Tap the stop button ■ to complete recording.

Customizing camera settings

On the preview screen, click the settings cog ⚙. Some options may be unavailable based on the shooting mode you're currently on.

Intelligent features

- **Scene optimizer**: Helps to adjust the color settings and apply the optimized effect automatically according to the subject or scene.
- **Scan QR codes**: Enables the device to scan QR codes from the preview screen.

Pictures

- **Swipe Shutter button to**: Choose what happens when you swipe the camera button to the edge of the screen and hold it.
- **Watermark**: Add a watermark at the lower left corner of the screen when capturing images.

Selfies

- **Save selfies as previewed**: Configure the device to save images as they appear on the preview screen when captured with the front camera without flipping them.

- **Swipe up/down to switch cameras**: When activated, this feature allows you switch cameras by swiping upwards and downwards on the preview screen.

Videos

- **High efficiency videos**: Record your videos in the High Efficiency Video Codec (HEVC) format. Your HEVC videos will be saved as compressed files to help you manage the device's memory.
- **Video stabilization**: Activate anti-shake to minimize or eliminate blurry image ensuing from camera shake while recording a video.

NOTE:

- You will not be able to play the HEVC videos on other devices or share them online.
- You will not be able to record Super slow motion and slow-motion videos in the HEVC format.

General

- **Auto HDR**: Capture images with rich colors and replicate details even in bright and dark areas.
- **Grid lines**: Show viewfinder guides to help composition when selecting subjects.

- **Location tags**: Attach a GPS location tag to the image.
  NOTE:
- GPS signal strength may reduce in places where the signal is obstructed, such as between buildings or in low-lying areas, or in poor weather conditions.
- Your location may show on your pictures when you upload them to the Internet. To prevent this, deactivate the location tag setting.
- **Shooting methods**: Select several more shooting methods for capturing an image or recording a video.
- **Settings to keep**: Preserve the last settings you used, such as the shooting mode, when you mount the camera.
- **Storage location**: Choose the memory location for storage. This feature will display when you insert a memory card.
- **Show Snapchat Licenses in Fun mode**: Automate the device to capture a photo with different effects with special unique Snapchat Lenses.

Privacy
- **Privacy Notice**: View the privacy notice.
- **Permissions**: View the permissions needed to operate the Camera app.

- **Reset settings**: Reset the camera settings.
- **About Camera**: Check the Camera app version and legal information.
- **Contact us**: Ask questions or see frequently asked questions.

Screenshotting and screen recording

You may want to take a screenshot while using your phone and then fondly annotate, illustrate, resize, or share the screenshot. This section will show you how all that is seamlessly possible.

How to capture a screenshot

Use the following simple approaches to capture a screenshot. You'll find your screenshots in **Gallery**.

Approach 1) Button capture: Press the Side button and the Volume Down button simultaneously.

Approach 2) Swipe capture: Swipe the edge of your hand to the left or right just across the device's screen.

NOTE:

- You'll not be able to capture a screenshot while using some apps and features.
- If capturing a screenshot by swiping is not yet activated in your device, launch the **Settings** app, tap **Ad-**

vanced features > Motions and gestures**, and then tap the **Palm swipe to capture** switch to activate it. After taking a screenshot, select from the following options on the toolbar at the bottom of the screen:

- ⌄ : Allows you to capture the current content and the hidden content on an extended page, such as a webpage. When you tap ⌄, the screen automatically scrolls down to capture more contents.

- ✎ : Enables you to write or draw on the screenshot or crop a section from the screenshot. You can then view the cropped area in **Gallery**.

- # : This will help you add some tags to the screenshot. To find screenshots by tag, tap the **Search** icon 🔍 in the **Gallery app**. There you'll see the tags list and quickly find any screenshot you're looking for.

- ⌳ : Lets you share the screenshot with others.

NOTE: If you do not see the options on the captured screen, simply go to the **Settings** app, tap **Advanced features > Screenshots and screen recorder**, and then tap the **Screenshot toolbar** switch to activate it. And there you are!

Screen record

Would you like to record the screen while using your device? Follow the simple steps:

1. Open the notification panel,
2. Swipe downwards,
3. Tap ◉ (**Screen recorder**) to activate it.
4. Choose a sound setting and tap **Start recording**. You'll have a countdown, after which recording will start.

    • If you want to write or draw on the screen, simply tap ✏.

    • If you to record a video of yourself, tap 👤

5. After recording the video, tap ■ to stop.

Your video will be automatically saved in **Gallery**.

NOTE: To modify the screen recorder settings, launch the **Settings** app and tap **Advanced features** > **Screenshots and screen recordings**.

Gallery

Here, you can explore images and videos stored in your phone. You can also manage images and videos according to album or create stories.

Using Gallery

Open the **Gallery** app to browse your images.

- More options
- Search for images and videos.
- Sync images and videos.

Viewing images

Launch the **Gallery** app and choose an image. To see other files, swipe to the left or right on the screen.

Image and video thumbnail

Modify the image.

Add the image to favourites.

Check details and additional features.

More options

Bixby Vision

View the content on a large screen using the Smart View feature.

Delete the image.

Share the image with others.

How to crop enlarged images in Gallery

1. Open the **Gallery** app and choose the image you want to crop.

2. Drag two fingers apart on the area you want to save and click ⊙.

The cropped area will automatically be saved for you as a file.

Viewing videos

Open the **Gallery** app and select a video to play. To view your other files, swipe to the left or right on the screen. To make use of several other options during playback, tap ⋮ , then tap **Open in Video player**.

View the content on a large screen using the Smart View feature.

Skip to the previous video. Touch and hold to rewind.

Rewind or fast-forward by dragging the bar.

Capture the current screen.

Create a GIF.

Change the screen ratio.

Configure the caption settings.

More options

Skip to the next video. Touch and hold to fast-forward.

Pause and resume playback.

Lock the playback screen.

Rotate the screen.

Change the playback speed.

Switch to the pop-up video player.

By dragging your finger up and down on the left side of the playback screen, you can adjust the playback's brightness, and by dragging it down the right side, you can adjust the playback's volume. To fast-forward or rewind the recording, swipe to the right or left on the playback screen.

Albums

Create albums and sort your images and videos.

1 To create an album, open the **Gallery** app, select **Albums,** tap the **Add** button ✛, and then select **Album**.
2 Select the items (images or videos) you wish to copy or move the images to an album.

Stories

As you take pictures or record videos and store them to the device, it will read the date and location tags on them, organize the pictures and videos, and then make stories out of them.

Launch the **Gallery** app, navigate to the **Stories** tab, and then choose a story to see. If you tap on the **More options** tab ⋮, you'll have access to a variety of choices, such as altering the content of the story or changing the title of the story.

You can create stories manually by tapping the stories list menu ⋮. and selecting **Create story** option.

How to Sync images and videos on your device with your cloud account

Open the **Gallery** app, click the **cloud** icon ☁, and then follow the on-screen instructions to finish the sync. The **Gallery** app will be synced with the cloud.

When your **Gallery** app is synced with the cloud, your pictures and videos will also be saved in the cloud. You can view images and videos saved in the cloud in your **Gallery** app and from other devices any time.

NOTE: When you have your Samsung account and Microsoft account connected, you can set the cloud storage as Microsoft OneDrive.

Deleting images or videos

Open the **Gallery** app, touch and hold an image, a video, or a story you want to delete, and then click **Delete**.

Using the recycle bin feature.

The recycle bin is a place in the phone where deleted images and videos can be temporarily kept for a certain period.

to activate this feature, open the **Gallery** app, click the **Menu** icon ≡, select **Settings**, and then tap the **Recycle bin** switch to on it.

To view files in the recycle bin, open the **Gallery** app and click ≡, and then **Recycle bin**.

AR Zone

Introduction

AR Zone offers you AR related features. Choose a feature and capture exciting pictures or videos.

Learn how to launch and use the AR Zone

Use the following procedures to launch AR Zone:

- Open the **AR Zone** app.

- Open your phone's **Camera** app and tap **MORE**, then select **AR ZONE**.

Learn about AR Emoji Studio

How to create AR Emoji

Create an emoji that looks like you thus:

1. Open the **AR Zone** app and click **AR Emoji Studio**.
2. Position your face straight on the screen, tap ⭕ to take a selfie or swipe to the left or right to see various pre-made emojis, select one and then tap ⮕.
3. Follow the on-screen commands to create an emoji.

You can select the AR emoji you want to use in the **AR Zone** app by selecting **AR Emoji Studio** > 〇≡ , and then selecting an emoji of your choice.

Deleting an emoji

Open the **AR Zone** app and click **AR Emoji Studio**, then click ⛾ and then the bin icon 🗑. Tick the emoji you want to delete, and finally, click **Delete**.

Making an AR emoji short video and using it to decorate your device.

You may utilize an emoji as a wallpaper or call background picture by making a short movie with it.

1. To access AR Emoji Studio, open the **AR Zone** app and select **AR Emoji Studio**.

2. Choose from three options: **Create video, Call screen**, or **Lock screen**.

3. Choose a template that you wish to use.

To change the background image, press 🔄 → 🖼.

4. To save the video, tap **Save**.

In the **Gallery**, you may see the videos you've saved.

5 Choose an option at the bottom of the screen to utilize the video immediately.

Using an AR emoji to create your contact profile.

Use an emoji as your Samsung account's profile image and in the **Contacts** app. You may select from a variety of postures or make your own.

1. Open the **AR Zone** app and select **AR Emoji Studio** from the menu.
2. Go to **Profile** and choose an emoji.
3. Choose a pose.
4. Tap the **Done** button, and then **Save**.

Working with AR Emoji Stickers

Make your own stickers with your emoji's expressions and actions. You will be able to use your emoji stickers when sending messages or use them on a social network.

Creating your own stickers

1. Open the **AR Zone** app and click **AR Emoji Stickers**.
2. Click ＋ at the top of the stickers list.
3. Edit stickers as you like and click **Save**.

   You can view the stickers you have made at the top of the stickers list.

Deleting emoji stickers

Open the **AR Zone** app and click **AR Emoji Stickers**→⋮ →**Edit**. Choose the emoji stickers to delete and click **Delete**.

How to use your emoji stickers in chats

You can use your emoji stickers when having a conversation through messages or on a social network. The underlisted actions are an example of using your emoji stickers in the **Messages** app.

1. During a message composition in the **Messages** app, click ☺ on the Samsung keyboard.
2. Tick the emoji icon.

3   Choose any of your emoji stickers.

The emoji sticker will be inserted into the message.

Emoji icon

Chapter Seven

GALAXY APPS AND FEATURES

Samsung Health

Samsung Health enables you manage your wellness and fitness. Define fitness goals, monitor your progress, and keep track of your overall wellness and fitness. You can also compare your step count records with other Samsung Health users and see other health tips. Please visit www.samsung.com/samsung-health for more details.

Using Samsung Health

Open the **Samsung Health** app. When you want to run this app for the first time or restart it after performing a data reset, use the on-screen guidelines to complete the setup.

To edit items on the Samsung Health home screen, click the **More options tab** ⋮ at the top right-hand corner of the screen, and select **Edit home**.

Monitor your health and fitness.

Compare your step count records with other Samsung Health users or compete with your friends.

Home cards

Manage your profile and view your health and fitness history.

View health tips.

Features of the Samsung Health app

- **Home:** The Home screen displays your health and fitness records for easy monitoring.

- **Together:** Here you can compare your step count records with other Samsung Health users or compete with friends.

- **Fitness:** This is where you get some health tips.

- **My page:** This is where you manage your profile and view your health and fitness history.

NOTE:

• Some features may be absent depending on the region.

- If you're using the steps tracker while travelling by car or train, your step count may affect your vibration.

Samsung Notes

Make notes by typing text from the keyboard or by handwriting or drawing on the screen. You can also insert your best-loved images or voice recordings into your notes.

Creating notes

1 Open the **Samsung Notes** app, click ⓒ, and then create a note.

You can change the input method by clicking ⓐ or ⓑ

Enter a title

Insert files

Reading mode

2 After composing the note, click the Back button to save it. If you want to save the note in another file format, touch ⁝→**Save as file**.

Deleting notes

Touch and hold a note to delete and click **Delete**.

Samsung Kids

You can restrict children's access to some apps, set their usage times, and configure settings to give an exciting and safe environment for children when they use the device.

Open the notification panel, swipe downwards, and then click 😊 (**Kids**) to activate the feature. The Samsung Kids screen will display. If it's not there, click the Edits menu button ✏, select **Edit,** and drag it over to add it. When you're using this feature for the first time or after performing a data reset, follow the on-screen instructions to complete the setup.

On the Samsung Kids screen, choose the app you want to use.

NOTE: Your preset screen lock method or your created PIN will be required when activating the **Parental controls** feature or closing Samsung Kids.

How to use the parental control features

You can configure the settings for Samsung Kids and check the usage history.

On the Samsung Kids screen, click ⋮→**Parental controls** and input your unlock code.

Closing Samsung Kids

To close Samsung Kids, click the Back button or click ⋮ →**Close Samsung Kids**, and then input your unlock code.

Galaxy Wearable

Galaxy Wearable is an app that lets you manage your wearable devices. When you connect your device to the wearable device, you can personalize the wearable device's settings and apps.

Open the **Galaxy Wearable** app.

Click the **More** > **Continue** to connect your device to the wearable device. Follow the on-screen instructions to finish the setup. Refer to the user manual of the specific wearable device for more information about how to connect and use it with your device.

Calendar

Manage your schedule by putting upcoming events in your planner.

Creating events

1   Open the **Calendar** app and click ⊕ or double-click a date.

If the date already has saved events or tasks in it, click the date, and click ⊕.

2   Enter event details and click **Save**.

Syncing events with your accounts

1   Open the **Settings** app, click **Accounts and backup** → **Manage accounts**, and then choose the account to sync with.

2   Click **Sync account** and click the **Calendar** switch to activate it.

To add accounts to sync with, open the **Calendar** app and click ≡→ ✿→**Manage calendars**. Then click thee plus button ✛ to add account. Then, choose an account to sync with and sign in. When you add an account, a blue circle is displayed next to the account name.

Reminder

Register to-do items as reminders and get notifications according to the condition you set.

NOTE:

- To receive more exact notifications, connect to a Wi-Fi or mobile network.

- To use location reminders, you must activate the GPS feature. Location reminders may be unavailable depending on the model.

Starting Reminder

Open the **Calendar** app and click the menu icon ≡, select **Reminder,** and then tap the **Add reminder** icon. The Reminder screen will display and the Reminder app icon () will be added to the Apps screen.

Creating reminders

1 Open the **Reminder** app.
2 Click **Write a reminder** or ⊕, input the details, and then click **Save**.

Completing reminders

On the reminders list click ○ or just choose a reminder and click **Complete**.

Restoring reminders

Restore reminders that have been completed.

1 On the reminders list, click the Menu tab ≡, and select **Completed**.
2 Mark items to restore and tap the **Restore** button.

When reminders are restored, they are included in the reminders list, and you will be reminded again.

Deleting reminders

To delete a reminder, choose a reminder and click **Delete**. To delete two or more reminders, touch and hold a reminder, tick the reminders to delete, and then tap **Delete**.

Voice Recorder

Record or play voice recordings.

1 Launch the **Voice Recorder** app.

2 Click ⬤ to start recording. Speak into the microphone.

- Click ⏸ to pause recording.

    - While making a voice recording, click **BOOKMARK** to insert a bookmark.

3 Click ⏹ to finish recording.

4 Type a file name and click **Save**.

Changing the recording mode on the Galaxy A15 5G

Choose a mode from the top of the voice recorder screen.

- **Standard**: This is the normal recording mode.
- **Speech-to-text**: The device records your voice and instantly converts it to on-screen text. For best results,

place the device close to your mouth and speak loudly and clearly in a place that is quiet.

NOTE: If the voice memo system language does not match the language you are speaking, the device will not recognize your voice. Before you use this feature, click the current language to set the voice memo system language.

How to listen to radio on your phone

Go to the Apps screen and tap the **Radio** app. Note however that the radio will not play unless you connect your headphones to the phone. The headphones serve as the radio antenna.

When you open the radio app with the headphones connected, the FM radio will automatically scan and save any available stations if that it's first time running.

- Enter radio frequency manually.
- Record audio from the FM radio.
- Turn the FM radio on or off.
- Fine-tune the frequency.
- Check the list of favourite stations.
- Now playing MHz
- Scan and save stations.
- More options
- Add the current station to the favourites list.
- Search for stations.
- Check the list of saved stations.

How to use the My Files app

Access and manage different files stored in the device.

Open the **My Files** app.

To search for unnecessary data and free up your device's storage, click **Analyze storage**. To search for files or folders, click Q.

Gaming Hub

Gaming Hub collects your games downloaded from **Play Store** and **Galaxy Store** into one place for seamless access. You can set the device to game mode to play games more easily.

Open the **Gaming Hub** app and choose the game you want.

NOTE:

- If **Gaming Hub** does not show, launch the **Settings** app, click **Advanced features**, and then click the **Gaming Hub** switch to activate it.
- Games downloaded from **Play Store** and **Galaxy Store** automatically show on the Gaming Hub screen. If you cannot see your games, then go to **My games**, tap the **More options** button ⋮, and select **Add games**.

Removing a game from Gaming Hub

Go to **My games,** touch and hold the game you want to remove, and then click **Remove**.

Changing the performance mode

You can change the game performance mode.

Open the **Gaming Hub** app, tap **More** → **Game Booster** → **Game optimization**, and then choose the mode you want.

- **Performance**: This focuses on providing you with the best possible performance while playing games.
- **Standard**: This helps to balance the performance and the battery usage time.
- **Battery saver**: This will help you save battery power while playing games.

NOTE: Efficiency of battery power may vary depending on the game.

Game Booster

Game Booster allows you to play games in a better environment. You can use Game Booster while playing games.

To open the Game Booster panel while playing games, click on the navigation bar. If the navigation bar does not show, drag upwards from the bottom of the screen to show it. If the navigation bar is set to use **Swipe gestures**, open the notification panel and click **Tap to open Game Booster.**

- ⚙ : Configure settings for Game Booster.
- 🔒 : Use this to lock the touch screen while playing game. To unlock, touch the screen and drag the lock icon in any direction on the screen.
- 📱 : This feature hides buttons on the navigation bar. You can bring up the buttons again on the screen by tapping 📱 on the navigation bar.
- 📷 : Take screenshots.
- ⏺ : For recording your game sessions. Tap ■ to stop recording.
- **Priority mode**: Set the device to block incoming calls and all notifications except for alarms so as to prevent any disturbance when playing your game.
- **Monitoring temperature / Monitoring memory**: Configure the device to automatically adjust settings to prevent overheating and to stop apps running in the background to better manage your device's memory.

- **Navigation button lock**: Hide the buttons on the navigation bar away from view. To display the buttons, click 🔒 on the navigation bar.
- **Screen touch lock**: Lock the touch screen while playing game. To unlock the touch screen, simply drag the lock icon in any direction.
- **Screenshot**: Capture screenshots.

NOTE:
- You can set to open the Game Booster panel from the navigation bar when the navigation bar is set to **Swipe gestures**. On the Game Booster panel, click ⚙ →**Block during game** and click the **Navigation gestures** switch to activate the feature.
- The options available may vary depending on the game.

Launching apps in pop-up windows while playing games

You can launch apps in pop-up windows even while playing a game.

Click ⚽ and select an app from the apps list.

Google apps

Google offers entertainment, social network, and business apps. You may need to have a Google account to access some apps.

To view more information about each app and access its help menu:

- **Chrome**: Search for information and browse web pages.
- **Gmail**: Sending or receiving emails via the Google Mail service.
- **Maps**: Find your exact location on the map, search the world map, and view information about you location and different places around you.
- **YT Music**: Enjoy yourself with different music and videos from YouTube Music. You can also view the music collections saved on your device and play them.
- **Play Movies & TV**: Purchase or rent videos, e.g. movies and TV programs, from **Play Store**.
- **Drive**: Store your content on the cloud, access it from anywhere and anytime, and share it with others.

- **YouTube**: Watch or create your own videos and share them with others.
- **Photos**: Search for, manage, and edit all your pictures and videos from different sources in one location.
- **Google**: Browse items on the Internet or your device.
- **Duo**: Make a simple video call.
- **Messages**: Send and receive messages on your device or computer, and share different types of content, e.g. images and videos.

NOTE: You may not find some apps, depending on the service provider or model.

Chapter Eight
CONNECTIONS AND SHARING

Wi-Fi

Activate the Wi-Fi feature to connect your device to a Wi-Fi network and be able to access the **Internet** or other network devices.

How to connect to a Wi-Fi network

1. On the Settings screen, click **Connections**, go to Wi-**Fi** and tap the switch to turn on the feature.
2. Choose a network from the Wi-Fi networks list. Networks with a lock icon means you need a password to connect to them.

NOTE:
- After the device has successfully connected to a Wi-Fi network for the first time, the device will reconnect to that network any other time it is available without requiring a password. To prevent the device from connecting to the network automatically, click ⚙ next to the network and click the **Auto reconnect** switch to deactivate it.

- If you're finding difficulty connecting to a Wi-Fi network properly, restart your device's Wi-Fi feature or the wireless router.

How to check the Wi-Fi network quality information

View the Wi-Fi network quality information, e.g. the speed and stability.

On the Settings screen, click **Connections** → **Wi-Fi** and click the switch to activate it. The network quality information will display under the Wi-Fi networks. If it does not display, click ⋮→**Intelligent Wi-Fi** and click the **Show network quality info** switch to activate it.

NOTE: The quality information may not show depending on the Wi-Fi network.

Wi-Fi Direct

Wi-Fi Direct connects devices directly via a Wi-Fi network without needing an access point.

1. On the Settings screen, click **Connections,** go to **Wi-Fi** and tap the switch to activate it.
2. Tap the **More options** tab ⋮, and select **Wi-Fi Direct**. The list of detected devices is displayed.

If the device you want to connect to is not shown on the list, request that the device turns on its Wi-Fi Direct feature.

3 Choose a device to connect to.

The devices will be connected when the other device accepts the request for Wi-Fi Direct connection.

To terminate the device connection, select the device to disconnect from the list.

Bluetooth

Use Bluetooth for exchange of data or media files with other Bluetooth-enabled devices.

Precautions for using Bluetooth:

- Samsung is not accountable for the loss, interception, or misuse of data sent or received via Bluetooth.
- Always make sure that you share and receive data with devices that are trusted and properly secured. If there are impediments between the devices, the operating distance may be reduced.
- Some devices may not be compatible with your device, especially those that are not tested or approved by the Bluetooth SIG.

- Never use the Bluetooth feature for illegal purposes (for example, pirating copies of files or illegally tapping communications for commercial purposes). Samsung will not take responsibility for the repercussion of illegal use of the Bluetooth feature.

How to pair your Galaxy A15 5G with other Bluetooth devices

1. On the **Settings** screen, click **Connections,** go to **Bluetooth,** and tap the switch to activate it. A list of the detected devices will pop up.
2. Choose a device to pair with.
   If the device you want to pair with is not displayed on the list, then set the device to enter Bluetooth pairing mode. Refer to the other user manual of the other device.
   NOTE: Your device will be visible to other devices while the Bluetooth settings screen is open.
3. Accept the Bluetooth connection request on your device to establish the connection.
   The devices become connected when the other device accepts the Bluetooth connection request.
   To unpair the devices, click ✱ next to the device name and click **Unpair**.

Sending and receiving data

Several apps support data transfer via Bluetooth. You can share data, such as contacts or media files, with other Bluetooth devices. The underlisted actions are an example of sending an image to another device.

1. Open the **Gallery** app and choose an image.
2. Tap ⤴ → **Bluetooth** and choose a device to transfer the image to.
   If the device you want to pair with is not in the list, request the device to turn on its visibility option.
3. Accept the request for Bluetooth connection on the other device.

NFC and contactless payments

Your device lets you read near field communication (NFC) tags that have information about products. You can also use this feature to make business transactions and purchase tickets for transportation or events after you have downloaded the relevant apps.

CAUTION: Your device contains a built-in NFC antenna. Handle the device with care to avoid damaging the NFC antenna.

Reading information from NFC tags

Make use of the NFC feature to read product information from NFC tags.

1 On the Settings screen, click **Connections** and click the **NFC and contactless payments** switch to activate it.

2 Place the NFC antenna area on the back of your device close to an NFC tag. The information from the tag will display on your phone. (See illustration)

NOTE: Make sure the device's screen is turned on and unlocked. If not, the device will not read NFC tags or receive data.

Making payments with the NFC feature

Before you can use the NFC feature to make payments, you must first register for the mobile payment service. If you want to register or get more information about the service, contact your service provider.

1. From the **Settings** screen, click **Connections** and click the **NFC and contactless payments** switch to activate the feature.
2. Use the NFC antenna area on the back of your device to touch the NFC card reader.

To set the default payment app, open the Settings screen and click **Connections** → **NFC and contactless payments** → **Contactless payments** → **Payment**, and then choose the app you want.

NOTE:
- All available payment apps may not be included in the payment services list.
- If you upgrade the payment app that you have been using or install a new one, it is possible that the payment services that you have been using in the past will no longer function properly. If this is the case, navigate to the **Settings** screen and choose **Connections**, followed by **NFC and contactless payments**, and then **Contactless payments** > **Payment** or **Others**, and then choose an alternative app to use instead of the one that was just updated or installed. Alternatively, deselect the app that has been chosen.

Data saver

Minimize your data usage by preventing some apps running in the background from sending or receiving data.

On the Settings screen, click **Connections** → **Data usage** → **Data saver** and click the switch to activate it.

When the data saver feature is activated, the icon will display on the status bar.

Data saver feature activated

To select apps to use data without restriction, click **Allowed to use data while Data saver is on** and select apps.

Allowed network for apps

Choose apps to always use the mobile data or Wi-Fi network, or both.

For instance, you can set the device to use only mobile data for apps that you want to keep secure or streaming apps that can be disconnected. Even though you do not deactivate the Wi-Fi feature, the apps will start using the mobile data.

On the Settings screen, click **Connections** → **Data usage** → **Allowed network for apps**, tap the switch to activate it, and then tap the other switches next to the apps you want.

NOTE: You may incur extra charges when using this feature.

Mobile Hotspot

To use your Galaxy A15 as a mobile hotspot to share its mobile data connection with other devices, follow these steps:

1. From the Settings screen, go to **Connections** → **Mobile Hotspot and Tethering** → **Mobile Hotspot**.
2. Turn on the Hotspot feature by tapping the switch. The Hotspot icon will appear on the status bar. You can reconfigure the level of security and the password by tapping **Configure**.
3. On the other device's screen, search for your phone's name from the Wi-Fi networks list and select it. Alternatively, click **QR code** on your phone's Mobile Hotspot screen and scan the QR code with the other device.

NOTE:

- If you can't find the mobile hotspot on your device, click **Configure** and set **Band** to **2.4 GHz**, click **Advanced**, and then click the **Hidden network** switch to turn it off.
- When you switch on the **Auto Hotspot** feature, you can share your device's mobile data connection with other devices signed in to your Samsung account.

More connection settings

Personalize settings to control other connection features.

From the Settings screen, click **Connections** → **More connection settings**.

- **Nearby device scanning**: Make the device to scan for nearby devices to connect to.
- **Printing**: Configure settings for printer plug-ins installed on your smartphone. You can search for available printers or add them manually to print files. Refer to Printing for further information.
- **VPN**: Set up virtual private networks (VPNs) on your smartphone to connect to a school or company's private network.
- **Private DNS**: Set your smartphone to use the security enhanced private DNS.

- **Ethernet**: As soon as you connect an Ethernet adaptor, you can use a wired network and configure network settings.

Printing

Configure settings for printer plug-ins installed on your smartphone. You can connect your smartphone to a printer via Wi-Fi or Wi-Fi Direct and print images or documents.

NOTE: Some printers may not be compatible with your smartphone.

Adding printer plug-ins

Add printer plug-ins for the printers that you want to connect your device to.

1. From the Settings screen, click **Connections** → **More connection settings** → **Printing** → **Download plugin**.
2. Choose a printer plug-in and install it.
3. Choose the installed printer plug-in.
   Your smartphone will automatically search for printers that are connected to the same Wi-Fi network as itself.
4. Pick a printer to add.

NOTE: To add printers manually, click ⋮ → **Add printer**.

How to print documents or images from your phone

While viewing content, such as images or documents, go to the options list, click **Print→▼→All printers...**, and then choose a printer.

NOTE: Printing methods may differ depending on the content type.

Different ways to share content on your Galaxy A15 smartphone.

Share content by using different sharing options. The actions listed below are an example of how you can share pictures.

1. Launch the **Gallery** app and choose a photo.

2. Tap the **Share** icon ⌃ and choose a sharing method you want.

NOTE: You may be charged extra when sharing files via the mobile network.

How to use the Quick Share

Sharing content with nearby devices

Share content with nearby devices using Wi-Fi Direct or Bluetooth, or with SmartThings supported devices.

1. Launch the **Gallery** app and choose an image.

2   On the other device, open the notification panel, swipe downwards, and then click⊚ (**Quick Share**) to activate the feature. If you don't find it there, click the Edits button ✏ and select **Edit,** and then drag it over to add it.

3   Tap the Share icon ◊ → **Quick Share** and choose a device to transfer the image to. If you want to share the link with a QR code, tap ▦ and scan the QR code.

4   Accept the request to transfer file on the other device.

NOTE: This feature is not supported when sharing videos with TVs or SmartThings supported devices. If you like watching videos on TV, then use the Smart View feature.

Sharing content with your contacts

With this method, you're able to share content with people saved in your contacts.

Step 1: Open the **Gallery** app and select the image you want to share.

Step 2: Click the **Share** button ◊, select **Quick Share,** and then select **View contact.**

Step 3: Select the contact you want to share with from your **Contacts** list.

How to use private sharing

With private sharing, you can share encrypted content with others and the recipients won't be able to save, copy, or resend such contents. This is a great way to share classified or confidential files.

To use private sharing, follow these steps:

Step 1
- Open the **Gallery** app and select an image you want to share.

Step 2
- Tap the **Share** icon and select **Quick Share.**
- Tap the **More options** icon and tap **Turn on Private sharing.**

Step 3
- Select the device you want to transfer the image to, or if its someone in your **Contacts,** tap **View contact**, and then select the contact.

Key: Share icon = ◁   More options = ⋮

Set who can find your phone.

Determine who is allowed to find and send content to your device.

1. Open the notification panel, swipe downwards, and then click ⊙ (**Quick Share**) to activate the feature.

You can also swipe down with two fingers from the Home screen and then click the **Quick Share** icon.

The Quick Share settings screen will be displayed.

2. Choose an option.
- **Non one**: Don't allow other people to find your device.
- **Contacts only**: Allow only those in your contacts to share with your device.
- **Anyone nearby**: Allow any neighboring devices to share with your device.

Music Share

The Music Share feature offers you the liberty to share your Bluetooth speaker that is already connected to your device with another person. You can also listen to the same music on your Galaxy Buds and someone else's Galaxy Buds.

You can get this feature only on devices that support the Music Share feature.

How to share your Bluetooth speaker with another device

You will be able to listen to music on your smartphone and someone else's smartphone via your Bluetooth speaker.

1. Ensure that your smartphone and your Bluetooth speaker are connected.
2. Go to **Settings** on your phone and tap **Connected devices**, then turn on the **Music Share** switch by tapping on it.

   You can explore more features, such as setting who to share your device with, by tapping **Music Share**.
3. On your friend's smartphone, choose your speaker from the list of the Bluetooth devices.
4. On your Galaxy A15 5G smartphone, accept the request for connection. When you do that, your speaker will be shared.

   When you play music via your friend's smartphone, the music playing via your smartphone will automatically be paused.

Listening to music together with Galaxy Buds

You can listen to music on your smartphone together via your Buds and your friend's Buds.

This feature is supported only on the Galaxy Buds series devices.

1. Ensure that your smartphone and your Bluetooth speaker are connected.

2. Go to **Settings** on your phone and tap **Connected devices,** ant turn on the **Music Share** switch by tapping on it.

   You can explore more features, such as setting who to share your device with, by tapping **Music Share**.

3. On your Galaxy A15 5G smartphone, open the notification panel and select **Media output**.

4. Tap **Music Sare** and choose your friend's Buds from the detected devices list.

5. On your friend's smartphone, accept the request to connect.

6. On your smartphone, mark your Buds and your friend's Buds on the audio output list.

   When you play music via your smartphone, both of you can listen to it together through your buds and your friend's.

SmartThings

Take charge of and manage smart appliances and Internet of Things (IoT) products with your smartphone.

To find more information, launch the **SmartThings** app and click the **Menu** tab ≡→**How to use**.

1   Launch the **SmartThings** app.
2   Tap **Devices**→✚ or tap **Add device**.
3   Choose a device and connect to it by following the on-screen instructions.

NOTE:

- Connection methods may vary according to the type of connected devices or the shared content.
- The devices you can connect vary by region. Available features may not be the same, depending on the connected device.

Connected devices' own errors or defects are not included in the Samsung warranty. If there are errors or defects on the connected devices, contact the device's manufacturer.

Smart View

View the content displayed on your device on a large screen by connecting your device to a screen mirroring-enabled TV or monitor.

1. Open the notification panel and swipe down, then click **Smart View**.

2. Choose a device to mirror your device's screen or display content.

NOTE: When you play a video with Smart View, the resolution may change depending on the TV model.

Chapter Nine
CUSTOMIZATION SETTINGS

Customize your smartphone to your needs by modifying its settings.

To access the settings, go to the Apps screen. The alternative is to pull down the notification panel and click the Settings icon ✱.

Use the **Search** button 🔍 to search for the settings you need by entering relevant keywords. In addition, you can look for settings by selecting a tag from the Suggestions menu.

Samsung account

Sign in to your Samsung account and manage it as desired.

On the Settings screen, click **Samsung account**.

Notifications

Change the notification settings.

On the Settings screen, click **Notifications**.

- **Notification pop-up style**: Choose a notification pop-up style and change the settings.

- **Do not disturb**: Configure your smartphone to mute all sounds apart from the allowed exceptions.

- **Advanced settings**: Configure advanced settings for notifications.

Display settings

Change the display and the Home screen settings.

On the Settings screen, click **Display**.

- **Light / Dark**: Activate or deactivate the dark mode feature.
- **Dark mode settings**: Reduce strain on your eye by applying the dark theme whenever you're using the device at night or in a dark place. You can set a schedule for when to apply dark mode.

NOTE:

The dark theme may not work in some apps.

- **Brightness**: Regulate the brightness of the display.
- **Adaptive brightness**: Make the device to keep up to date with your brightness adjustments and apply them automatically in similar lighting conditions.
- **Motion smoothness**: Modify the refresh rate of the screen. When you set high refresh rate, the screen will scroll more smoothly and seamlessly. Refer to Motion smoothness for further information.

- **Eye comfort shield**: Reduce eye strain by reducing the amount of blue light that is emitted by the screen. You can set a plan for applying this feature.
- **Screen mode**: Change the screen mode to regulate the display's color and contrast. Refer to Changing the screen mode or adjusting the display color for further information.
- **Font size and style**: Modify the font size and style.
- **Screen zoom**: Make the items on the screen bigger or smaller.
- **Full screen apps**: Choose apps to use with the full screen aspect ratio.
- **Screen timeout**: Set how long the device waits before turning off the display's backlight.
- **Easy mode**: Switch to easy mode to show larger icons and apply a simpler layout to the Home screen.
- **Edge panels**: Modify the settings for the Edge panel.
- **Navigation bar**: Change the navigation bar settings. Refer to Navigation bar (soft buttons) for further information.
- **Accidental touch protection**: Make the device's screen not detect any touch input when it is in a dark place, such as a pocket or bag.

- **Touch sensitivity**: Increase the touch sensitivity of the screen when used with screen protectors.
- **Show charging information**: Set the device to show the charging information, such as the remaining battery percentage when the screen is off.
- **Screen saver**: Set the device to start a screen saver when the device is charging.

NOTE: Some features may not be found depending on the model.

Home screen

Configure your personal settings for the Home screen, such as the screen layout.

Open the **Settings** screen menu, click **Home screen**.

Motion smoothness

The refresh rate refers to the number of times the screen is refreshed every second. Use a high refresh rate so that the screen does not glimmer when switching between screens. The screen will scroll more smoothly. Your battery usage will reduce when you select a standard refresh rate, meaning you can use the battery longer.

1 On the Settings screen, click **Display** → **Motion smoothness**.

2   Choose a refresh rate.

- **Adaptive**: Experience a smooth animation and scrolling by automatically regulating your screen refresh rate up to 120 Hz.
- **Standard**: Use a standard refresh rate in normal situations to reduce battery power consumption.

How to change the screen mode or adjust the display color:

Change the screen mode or adjust the display color to your favorite.

Changing the screen mode

On the Settings screen, click **Display** → **Screen mode** and choose a mode you want.

- **Vivid**: This enhances the color range, saturation, as well as the sharpness of your display. You can also alter the display color balance by color value.
- **Natural**: This alters the screen to a natural tone.

NOTE: You cannot adjust the display color except in **Vivid** mode.

- **Vivid** mode may not function well with third-party apps.

Optimizing the full screen color balance

improve the display color by adjusting the color tones to your own preference. On the Settings screen, click **Display** → **Screen mode** → **Vivid** and fine-tune the color adjustment bar under **White balance**.

When you pull the color adjustment bar towards **Cool**, the blue color tone will increase. When you pull the bar towards **Warm**, the red color tone will increase.

Adjusting the screen tone by color value

Increase or lower certain color tones by modifying the Red, Green, or Blue value individually.

1 On the Settings screen, click **Display** → **Screen mode** → **Vivid**.

2 Tap **Advanced settings**.

3 Adjust the **R** (Red), **G** (Green), or **B** (Blue) color bar as desired. The screen tone will be adjusted.

Wallpaper

Change the wallpaper settings for the Home screen and the locked screen. Once in **Settings,** click **Wallpaper and style**.

Themes

Apply different themes to your smartphone to change the visual elements of the Home screen, locked screen, and icons. From the **Settings** screen menu, click **Themes**.

Sounds and vibration

Options

Change settings for different sounds on the device.

On the Settings screen, clicks **Sounds and vibration**.

- **Sound mode**: Make the device to use sound mode, vibration mode, or silent mode.

- **Vibrate while ringing**: Make the device to vibrate and play a ringtone for incoming calls.

- **Temporary mute**: Make the device to use silent mode for a certain period.

- **Ringtone**: Change the call ringtone.

- **Notification sound**: Change the notification sound.

- **System sound**: Alter the sound to use for some kinds of actions, such as charging the device.
- **Volume**: Regulate the device's volume level.
- **Call vibration pattern**: Change the call vibration pattern.
- **Notification vibration pattern**: Change the notification vibration pattern.
- **Vibration intensity**: Regulate the force of the vibration notification.
- **System sound/vibration control**: Make the device to sound or vibrate for actions, such as controlling the touch screen.
- **Sound quality and effects**: Set the sound quality and effects of the device. Refer to Sound quality and effects for further information.
- **Separate app sound**: Make the device to play media sound from a specific app separately on the other audio device. Refer to Separate app sound for further information.

NOTE:Some features may be unavailable depending on the model.

Sound quality and effects.

Set the device's sound quality and effects.

On the Settings screen, click **Sounds and vibration** → **Sound quality and effects**.

- **Dolby Atmos**: Choose a surround sound mode optimized for different types of audios, such as movies, music, and voice. Using Dolby Atmos, you can experience moving audio sounds that flow all around you.

- **Dolby Atmos for gaming**: Experience the Dolby Atmos sound optimized for games as you play games.

- **Equalizer**: Choose an option for a specific music genre and enjoy optimized sound.

- **UHQ upscaler**: Increase the sound resolution of music and videos.

- **Adapt sound**: Make the best sound for you.

NOTE: Subject to the model, you must connect an earphone to use some features.

Separate app sound

Make the device to play media sound from a specific app on the connected Bluetooth speaker or headset.

For example, you can listen to the Navigation app through your device's speaker while at the same time listening to playback from the Music app through the vehicle's Bluetooth speaker.

1. On the Settings screen, click **Sounds and vibration** → **Separate app sound** and click the switch to activate it.
2. Choose an app to play media sounds separately and click the Back button.
3. Choose a device for playing the chosen app's media sound.

Chapter Ten
ACCOUNTS AND BACKUP

Sync, back up, or restore your smartphone's data using Samsung Cloud. You can also sign in to accounts, such as your Samsung account or Google account, or transfer data to or from other devices by using Smart Switch.

On the Settings screen, click **Accounts and backup**.

- **Manage accounts**: Add your Samsung and Google accounts, or other accounts, to sync with.
- **Samsung Cloud**: Back up your data and settings, and restore the previous device's data and settings even when you do not have it. Refer to Samsung Cloud for further information.
- **Google Drive**: Keep your personal information, app data, and settings safe on your smartphone. You can back up your sensitive information. You must have to sign in to your Google account to back up data.
- **Smart Switch**: Launch Smart Switch and transfer data from your old device. Refer to *Transferring data from your previous device (Smart Switch)* for additional information.

NOTE: Back up your data often to a safe location, such as Samsung Cloud or a computer, so that you can restore it if the data is corrupted or lost due to an accidental factory data reset.

Samsung Cloud

Back up your smartphone's data to Samsung Cloud and restore it later.

Backing up data to Samsung Cloud

You can back up your smartphone's data to Samsung Cloud.

1 From the Settings screen, click **Accounts and backup** and click **Back up data** under **Samsung Cloud**.

2 Mark items you want to back up and click **Back up now**.

3 Click the **Done** button.

NOTE:

- All your data will not be backed up. To check which data will be backed up, on the Settings screen, click **Accounts and backup** > **Back up data** under the **Samsung Cloud** section.

- To check the backup data for other devices in your Samsung Cloud, navigate to the **Settings** screen, click

Accounts and backup → **Restore data**, and then choose a device you want.

Restoring data

You can restore your backup data from Samsung Cloud to your smartphone.

1 From the Settings screen, click **Accounts and backup**.
2 Click **Restore data** and choose a device you want.
3 Mark items you want to restore and click **Restore**.

Chapter Eleven
ADVANCED SETTINGS

Advanced features

Activate advanced features and modify the settings that control each feature.

From the Settings screen, click **Advanced features**.

- **Call & text on other devices**: Use your device's calling and messaging features on other devices that are signed in to your Samsung account.

- **Continue apps on other devices**: Use your device's apps on other devices that are signed in to your Samsung account.

- **Link to Windows**: Promptly access data saved in your device on your computer. See the section on *Link to Windows* for further details.

- **Android Auto**: Connect your device to a vehicle and control some of your device's features on the vehicle's display.

- **Side key**: Select an app or feature to start using the Side key. Refer to *Setting the Side key* for further information.

- **Motions and gestures**: Activate the motion feature and organize settings. Refer to *Motions and gestures* for additional information.

- **One-handed mode**: Activate one-handed operation mode for your convenience when using the smartphone with one hand.
- **Bixby Routines**: Add routines to automate settings that you use frequently. Your smartphone also recommends useful routines according to your frequent activities. Refer to *Bixby Routines* for additional information.
- **Screenshots and screen recorder**: Modify the settings for screenshots and screen recorder.
- **Show contacts when sharing content**: Make the device to display the people you contacted on the sharing options panel to let you share content directly.
- **Dual Messenger**: Install the second app. Use two distinct accounts for the same messenger app. Refer to *Dual Messenger* for more details.

NOTE: Some features may be unavailable depending on the service provider or model.

Motions and gestures

Activate the motion feature and configure settings.

From the Settings screen, click **Advanced features** → **Motions and gestures**.

- **Lift to wake**: Make the device to turn on the screen anytime you pick it up.
- **Double tap to turn on screen**: Make the device to turn on the screen by double-tapping anywhere on the screen while it's turned off.

- **Double tap to turn off screen**: Make the device to turn off the screen when you double-tap an empty area on the Home screen or the locked screen.
- **Keep screen on while viewing**: Make the device to stop the display from turning off while you are looking at it.
- **Alert when phone picked up**: Make the device to prompt you if you have missed calls or new messages whenever you pick up the device.

  NOTE: This feature may not respond if the device's screen is turned on or the device is not placed on a flat surface.
- **Mute with gestures**: Make the device to mute some kind of sounds by using motions or gestures.
- **Palm swipe to capture**: Make the device to capture a screenshot when you swipe your hand to the left or right across the screen. You can view the captured images in your device's **Gallery**. Some apps and features will not allow you to capture a screenshot while using them.

NOTE: Excessive shaking or an impact to the device may cause an input that is not intended in situations of some features using sensors.

Video call effects

During video calls, you may use several options such as altering the background.

Press Advanced features, then Video call effects while on the Settings screen, then tap the switch to turn it on. The ◉ icon will be placed to the screen of the video calling app.

Making use of video call effects

Tap ◉ on the screen of the video calling app.

• Reset all: Reset all the settings.

• Background: During video calls, change or blur the background.

• Auto framing: Turn on or off the feature of auto framing. When you enable this function, the device adjusts the filming angle and zoom automatically during video conversations by recognizing and tracking individuals.

• Settings: Choose from a variety of backdrop colors and graphics to use during video conversations.

NOTE:

• Depending on the model, some functionalities may be unavailable.

• Some functionalities are only available when the front camera is used.

Dual Messenger

Install another app and use two distinct accounts for the same messenger app.

1 From the Settings screen, click **Advanced features → Dual Messenger**.

   Supported apps will show.

2 Click the switch of an app to install the second app and you will have it installed. The second app's icon will be shown with ⊙.

— Second app

NOTE:

- Depending on the app, the Dual Messenger feature may not be available.
- The second app may have limited features.

Uninstalling a second app

1 From the Settings screen, click **Advanced features** → **Dual Messenger**.

2 Click the switch of the app you want to uninstall and click **Uninstall**. Every data relating to the second app will be deleted from the device.

NOTE: If the first app is uninstalled, the second app will also be deleted.

Digital Wellbeing and parental controls

View the history of your device usage and use features to stop your device from meddling with your life. You may also like to set up parental controls for your children and manage their digital use.

From the Settings screen, click **Digital Wellbeing and parental controls**.

- **Screen time**: Set goals for how much you use your device daily.
- **App timers**: Limit each app's daily usage time by setting a timer. When you get to the limit, the app will be deactivated, and you will not be able to use it more.
- **Focus mode**: Activate focus mode. This helps you to avoid distractions from your device and stay focused on what you want. You can allow some apps to be used in focus mode.
- **Bedtime mode**: Activate bedtime mode to reduce eye strain before you go to sleep and prevent you from being disturbed while sleeping.
- **Parental controls**: Take charge of your children's digital use.

Battery and device care

The device care feature gives you a summary of the position of your device's battery, storage, memory, and system security. You are also able to automatically optimize the device by simply tapping with your finger.

Optimizing your device

From the Settings screen, click **Battery and device care → Optimize now**.

The quick optimization feature enhances the device performance through the following means:

- Helping to close apps that may be running in the background.
- Managing unusual battery usage.

- Scanning for any crashed apps and malware in your device.

How to use the auto optimization feature

Your device can be set to perform auto optimization when it is not in use. In **Settings,** click **Device care > Optimize now.** The quick optimization feature helps to enhance your device's performance through the following ways:

- By closing apps that are running in the background.
- By managing unusual battery usage.
- Scanning for crashed apps and malware.

Battery

Check the remaining battery power and how long you can use the device. If your devices have low battery level, conserve battery power by activating power saving features.

From the Settings screen, click **Device care → Battery.**

- **Power saving mode**: Activate power saving mode to lengthen the battery's usage time.

- **Background usage limits**: Limit battery usage for apps that you do not use frequently.

- **More battery settings**: Configure advanced battery settings.

NOTE:

- The usage time left shows how long more you can use the device before the battery power runs out. Usage time left may by device settings and operating conditions.

- You may not receive notifications from some apps when using power saving mode.

Storage

Check the status of the used memory as well as the available memory.

From the Settings screen, click **Device care** → **Storage**. To delete files or uninstall apps that you no longer use, choose a category. Then, click and hold, or choose an item and click **Delete** or **Uninstall**.

NOTE:

- The actual available capacity of the internal memory is usually less than the stated capacity. This is because the operating system and default apps occupy part of the memory.

  The available capacity may change still anytime you update the device.
- To view the available capacity of the internal memory, access the Specification section for your device on the Samsung website.

Memory

From the Settings screen, click **Device care** → **Memory**.

To speed up your device by stopping apps running in the background, mark apps from the apps list, and click **Clean now**.

App protection

Check the security status of your device. This feature helps to scan your device for malware.

From the Settings screen, click **Device care** → **App protection** → **Scan phone**.

Maintenance mode

To maintain your privacy while another person is using your device, such as when you send it in for repairs, you should safeguard it by activating the maintenance mode.

You can activate maintenance mode from the **Settings** screen by selecting **Device care** > **Maintenance mode** > **Turn on**.

How to use the Ultra data saving mode

You may control and limit your mobile data consumption by blocking apps from accessing the connection when they are in the background. You may also compress internet data, such as photos, movies, and webpages, that you access over the mobile network by making use of the data compression tool.

To activate Ultra data saving, go to the **Settings** menu, then select **Device care** and toggle on the corresponding switch.

• This function might not be accessible depending on the mobile network you use or the device you purchase. When this function is activated, it is possible that certain web sites or content will not be accessible due to limitations imposed by the service provider or the constraints of the mobile network.

Apps

Manage the apps in your device and change their settings. You can view the apps' usage information, change their notification or permission settings, or uninstall or disable any unnecessary apps.

From the Settings screen, click **Apps**.

General management

Personalize your device's system settings or reset the device.

From the Settings screen, click **General management**.

- **Language**: Choose device languages. Refer to *Adding device languages* for more details.

- **Text-to-speech output**: Change the settings for text-to-speech features to make use of when you activate TalkBack. For instance, you can modify languages, speed, and more.

- **Date and time**: Access and modify the settings to control how your device displays the time and date.

  NOTE:If the battery becomes completely discharged, the time and date is reset.

- **Samsung Keyboard settings**: Alter the settings for the Samsung keyboard.

- **Keyboard list and default**: Choose a keyboard to use by default and alter the keyboard settings.

- **Physical keyboard**: Alter the settings for an external keyboard.
- **Mouse and trackpad**: Alter the settings for an external mouse or trackpad.
- **Autofill service**: Choose an autofill service to use.
- **Reset**: Reset the settings of your device or execute a factory data reset.
- **Contact us**: Make an enquiry or view frequently asked questions.

Adding device languages

Add more languages to use on your device.

1 From your Settings screen, click **General management** → **Language** → **Add language**. If you like to view all the languages you can possibly add, click⁝→**All languages**.

2 Choose a language to add.

3 To set the chosen language as the default language, click **Set as default**. To retain the current language setting, click **Keep current**.

The chosen language will be added to your languages list. If you have modified the default language, the chosen language will be added to the top of the list.

To alter the default language from your languages list, choose the language you want and click**Apply**. If there's any app that doesn't support the default language, the next supported language in the list will be used instead.

Accessibility

Configure various settings in your device to improve its accessibility.

From the Settings screen, click **Accessibility**.

- **Recommended for you**: Find out about the accessibility features you are currently using and see other recommended features you may like.
- **TalkBack**: Activate TalkBack, which offers you voice feedback. To view help information to know more about how you can use this feature, click **Settings → TalkBack tutorial**.
- **Visibility enhancements**: Personalize the settings to improve accessibility for users with impaired vision.
- **Hearing enhancements**: Personalize the settings to enhance accessibility for users with hearing impairment.
- **Interaction and dexterity**: Personalize the settings to enhance accessibility for users who have low dexterity.
- **Advanced settings**: Configure settings concerning Direct access and notification features.
- **Installed services**: View accessibility services installed on your smartphone.
- **About Accessibility**: Check the Accessibility information.
- **Contact us**: Make enquiry or view frequently asked questions.

Software update

Update the software of your smartphone through the firmware over-the-air (FOTA) service. You can also plan software updates.

From the Settings screen, click **Software update**.

- **Download and install**: Find out about updates and install them manually.
- **Auto download over Wi-Fi**: Make the device to download updates automatically whenever it's connected to a Wi-Fi network.
- **Last update**: Review information about the last software update.

NOTE:

Whenever there are emergency software updates which are meant to secure your device and to block new types of security threats, they will be installed automatically without your consent.

Security updates information

Security updates are meant to strengthen the security of your device and protect your personal information from external threats. For security updates for your device's model, visit *security.samsungmobile.com*.

NOTE:The website does not support all languages.

About phone

Access useful information about your device.

From the Settings screen, click **About phone**.

To modify your device's name, click **Edit**.

- **Status information**: Look at several device information, such as the SIM card status, Wi-Fi MAC address, and serial number.

- **Legal information**: Access legal information concerning the device, such as safety information and the opensource license.

- **Software information**: See the software information of your smartphone, such as the versions of its operating system and firmware.

- **Battery information**: Show the device's battery status and information.

Chapter Twelve
TROUBLESHOOTING TIPS

Before you eventually contact a Samsung Service Centre, please try the following solutions, although some conditions may not apply to your device.

You may also find Samsung Members handy to solve any problems you might experience while using your device.

When your device prompts you to enter one of the following codes while using it or when you turn on the device:

- Password: If you have enabled the device lock feature, you must enter the password you set for the device.

- PIN: When you want to use your smartphone for the first time or when you enable the PIN requirement, you must enter the PIN supplied with the SIM or USIM card. However, you can disable the feature by simply using the Lock SIM card menu.

- PUK: This means your SIM or USIM card has been blocked, usually because you have entered your PIN incorrectly several times. You must enter the PUK supplied with SIM or USIM card by your service provider.

- PIN2: When you access a menu that needs the PIN2, you must enter the PIN2 supplied with the SIM or USIM card. For more information about this issue, contact your service provider.

If your device is showing network or service error messages

- This usually happens because of weak signals or poor reception, making your device to lose reception. Try move away from your current area to another area. While moving, error messages may show again severally.
- You need a subscription to access some options in your device or its apps. For further information, contact your service provider.

Your phone refuses to turn on.

When the battery is utterly discharged, your device will not turn on. Charge the battery fully before turning on the device.

The touchscreen does not respond properly or is responding slowly.

- This may be because of a screen protector, or other optional accessories attached to the touchscreen.
- If you're putting on hand gloves, if your hands are not clean while touching the touchscreen, or if you're tapping the screen with your fingertips or with sharp objects, the touchscreen may not function properly.
- The touchscreen may not function well in humid conditions or when it is exposed to water. So ensure the touchscreen is clean and dry.
- Restart your device to be sure it's cleared of any temporary software bugs.
- Confirm that your device software is updated to the latest version.

- If you have your device's touchscreen scratched or damaged, visit a Samsung Service Centre.

Your device freezes or experiences a fatal error.

Experiment the following solutions. If the problem persists, contact a Samsung Service Centre.

Restarting the device

If your device is freezing or hanging intermittently, you may need to close all open apps or turn off the device and turn it on again.

Forcing restart

If your device is frozen and unresponsive, press and hold the Side key and the Volume Down key together at the same time for more than 7 seconds to restart it.

Resetting the device

If the methods above do not solve your problem, do a factory data reset.

Start the **Settings** app and click **General management** → **Reset** → **Factory data reset** → **Reset** → **Delete all**. Before performing the factory data reset, make sure you have a backup copy of important data stored in your device.

Calls are not connected.

- Confirm that you have accessed the right cellular network.
- Check if you have set call barring for the phone number you are dialing. If you have done so, your call will not connect.

- Confirm that you have not set call barring for the incoming phone number.

Others cannot hear you when making a call.

- Make sure that you do not cover the built-in microphone by any means.
- Make sure that you place the microphone close to your mouth.
- If you're using headphones, make sure that they are properly connected.

You hear sound echoes during a call.

Regulate the volume by pressing the Volume key or move to another area.

A cellular network or the Internet is frequently disconnected or poor audio quality.

- Make sure that you're not blocking the device's internal antenna.
- When you are in areas where there are weak signals or poor reception, you may lose reception. Problems of connectivity may be associated with the service provider's base station. Change your location and try again.
- When you are using the device while moving, wireless network services may be disabled because of problems with the service provider's network.

The battery doesn't charge well (For Samsung-approved chargers)

- Make sure the charger is connected properly.

- Visit a Samsung Service Centre for a replacement of the battery.

The battery depletes faster than when you first purchased it.

- Exposure of the device or the battery to very cold or very hot temperatures, may reduce the useful charge.
- Consider the apps and other features you use. Battery consumption increases with certain features or apps, such as GPS, games, or the Internet.
- The battery is expendable, and the useful charge reduces over time. Consider replacing your expended battery.

Error messages pop up when launching the camera.

You must have enough available memory and battery power to operate the camera app. If you get error messages when starting the camera, try the following:

- Charge the battery.
- Free up some space in your memory by transferring files to a computer or deleting files from your device.
- Restart the device. If the problem persists with the camera app after trying these tips, contact a Samsung Service Centre.

Picture quality is poorer than the preview.

- The quality of your pictures depends on the surroundings and the photography techniques you apply.
- Taking pictures in dark areas, at night, or indoors may cause image noise or make images to be captured out of focus.

Error messages pop up when opening multimedia files.

If you receive error messages or you're unable to play multimedia files on your device, try the following:

- Free up some space in your device memory by transferring files to a computer or deleting files from your device.
- Check if the music file is Digital Rights Management (DRM)-protected. If it is, you must provide the appropriate license or key to play the file.
- Make sure that the file formats are supported by your device. If the file format is not supported, such as DivX or AC3, install the relevant app that supports it. To check the file formats that your device supports, visit the Samsung website.
- Your device supports pictures and videos that are captured with it. Pictures and videos captured by other devices may not be supported.
- Your device supports multimedia files that are authenticated by your network service provider or providers of additional services. You may have problems working with some content from the Internet, such as ringtones, videos, or wallpapers.

Bluetooth is not working well.

Another Bluetooth device may be located or there may be connection problems or performance malfunctions. Otherwise, try the following:

- Make sure the device you want to connect with is ready to be scanned or connected to.
- Make sure that your device and the other Bluetooth device are within the maximum Bluetooth range which is 10m.
- On your device, start the **Settings** app, click **Connections**, and then click the **Bluetooth** switch to activate again.
- On your device, start the **Settings** app, click **General management** → **Reset** → **Reset network settings** → **Reset settings** → **Reset** to reset network settings. Your registered information may be lost when performing the reset.

If the above tips do not resolve the problem, contact a Samsung Service Centre.

The screen brightness adjustment bar does not show on the notification panel.

Open the notification panel by pulling the status bar downwards, and then pull the notification panel downwards. Click ⋮ → **Quick panel layout** and click the **Show brightness control above notifications** switch to activate it.

Unable to establish a connection when you connect the device to a computer.

- Make sure you are using a compatible USB cable with your device.

- Make sure you have the proper driver installed on your computer and that it's up to date.

Your device cannot find your current location.

GPS signals may be obstructed by buildings or other conditions in some locations. In such circumstances, set the device to use Wi-Fi or a mobile network to find your current location.

Data stored in the device has been lost.

Always have a backup copy of every important data stored in the device. Otherwise, you cannot bring back your data if it is corrupted or lost. Samsung will not be held accountable for the loss of data stored in the device.

A small gap shows around the outside of the device case.

- This gap is an essential manufacturing feature, and some slight rocking or vibration of parts may take place.
- With the lapse of time, friction between parts may lead to slight expansion of this gap.

There is insufficient space in the device's storage.

Delete any redundant data, such as cache, by making use of the device care feature or you can manually delete fallow apps or files to free up storage space.

The Home button does not appear.

The navigation bar which contains the Home button may disappear when using some apps or features. To view the navigation bar, pull upwards from the bottom of the screen.

Removing the battery

- If you want to remove the battery for any reason, contact an authorized service center. To get instructions on how to remove battery, please visit **www.samsung.com/global/ecodesign_energy**.

- For your safety, you **must not try to remove** the battery by yourself. If the battery is not properly removed, it may result in damage to the battery and/or device, cause personal injury, and/or result in the device being unsafe to use.

- Samsung does not accept any legal responsibility for any damage or loss (whether in contract or tort, including negligence) which may ensue from failure to exactly follow these warnings and instructions, save for death or personal injury caused by Samsung's negligence.

INDEX

About phone, **171**
Accessibility, **170**
Add contacts, **70**
Albums, **104**
App permission, **29**
Apps screen, **53**
AR Emoji Stickers, **110**
AR Emoji Studio, **107**
AR Zone, **106**
Back up, **26**
Backup, **156**
backup data, **26**
Battery, **164**, **165**, **181**
Block numbers, **67**
Bluetooth, **129**
Calendar, **116**
Camera, **80**
Care, **164**
Copy, **74**
Copying and pasting, **74**
Create folders, **57**
Data saver, **134**
Delete contacts, **71**

Delete folder, **58**
Deleting images, **106**
Digital Wellbeing, **163**
Display, **147**, **150**
Edge panel, **59**
Emergency call, **19**
Emergency mode, **19**
Emoji, **107**
Face recognition, **30**
Files, **121**
Fingerprint, **33**
Fingerprint recognition, **33**
Food mode, **93**
Forcing restart, **19**, **175**
Fun mode, **90**
Galaxy, **116**
Galaxy Store, **27**
Galaxy Wearable, **116**
Gallery, **101**
Game, **122**
Google apps, **125**
Home screen, **53**, **149**

Hotspot, **135**
Hyperlapse, **95**
ID, **22**
Indicator icons, **60**
Intelligent features, **96**
Internet, **77**
Keyboard, **73**
Keyboard functions, **75**
Lock screen, **59**
Macro mode, **94**
Making calls, **65**
Media playback, **64**
Memory, **166**
Messages, **72**
Messenger, **162**
Mobile Hotspot, **135**
Motions and gestures, **160**
Music Share, **141**
Nano-SIM card, **10**
Navigation bar. *See* Soft buttons
NFC, **131**
Night mode, **93**
Notifications, **146**

Panorama mode, **93**
Parental control, **115**
Parental controls, **163**
Paste, **75**
Photo mode, **87**
Play Store, **28**
Portrait mode, **89**
Printing, **137**
Pro mode, **91**
Quick setting, **63**
Quick Share, **138**
Receiving calls, **67**
Recorder, **119**
Reminder, **117**
Restart, **19**
Restarting, **175**
Samsung account, **21**, **22**, **46**, **146**
Samsung Cloud, **157**
Samsung Health, **112**
Samsung Kids, **115**
Samsung Notes, **114**
Samsung Pass, **46**
Screen record, **101**
Screenshot, **99**
SD card, **14**
Secure Folder, **39**, **42**

Secure Wi-Fi, **44**
Selfies, **88**, **96**
Setup, **21**
Share, **138**, **141**
Sharing contacts, **72**
SIM card, **13**
Slow motion, **94**
Smart Lock, **38**
Smart Switch, **23**
SmartThings, **143**
Soft buttons, **52**
Soundechoes, **176**
Sounds and vibration, **152**

Storage, **166**
Syncing, **105**
Transferring data. *See* Smart switch
Troubleshooting, **173**
Uninstall, **28**
Update, **171**
USIM card. *See* Nano-SIM card
Video call effects, **161**
Wearable, **116**
Wi-Fi, **127**
Wi-Fi Direct, **128**

Printed in Great Britain
by Amazon